MW01533981

$2⁵⁰ x

SIOUX TRAIL

Among Other Books by John Upton Terrell

INDIAN WOMEN OF THE WESTERN MORNING
(with Donna M. Terrell)
PUEBLOS, GODS AND SPANIARDS
LAND GRAB
APACHE CHRONICLE
AMERICAN INDIAN ALMANAC
BUNKHOUSE PAPERS
THE NAVAJO
THE MAN WHO REDISCOVERED AMERICA
THE SIX TURNINGS
LA SALLE
ZEBULON PIKE
ESTEVANICO THE BLACK
TRADERS OF THE WESTERN MORNING
FAINT THE TRUMPET SOUNDS
PUEBLO DE LOS CORAZONES
WAR FOR THE COLORADO RIVER
BLACK ROBE
FURS BY ASTOR
JOURNEY INTO DARKNESS
PLUME ROUGE
SUNDAY IS THE DAY YOU REST
ADAM CARGO
THE LITTLE DARK MAN

SIOUX TRAIL

John Upton Terrell

McGRAW-HILL BOOK COMPANY
New York   St. Louis   San Francisco
Düsseldorf   Mexico   Toronto

Book designed by Elaine Gongora.

Copyright © 1974 by John Upton Terrell.
All rights reserved. Printed in the United
States of America. No part of this publication
may be reproduced, stored in a retrieval system,
or transmitted, in any form or by any means,
electronic, mechanical, photocopying, recording,
or otherwise, without the prior written permission
of the publisher.

123456789BABA7987654

Library of Congress Cataloging in Publication Data

Terrell, John Upton, date
    Sioux trail.

    1. Dakota Indians.   I.   Title.
E99.D1T29   970.3   74-5299
ISBN 0-07-063685-0

CONTENTS

AUTHOR'S NOTE

The people we call Sioux are generally thought of, and usually portrayed, as fierce fighters of the Western buffalo plains, in magnificent painted buckskins and streaming feather bonnets dashing on their horses into battle. They were that, but not for long . . . actually only in the eighteenth and nineteenth centuries.

Sioux was not the name by which they identified themselves when white men first encountered them. Indeed, *sioux* is not a word of their language. Their ancient antagonists, the Algonquian Chippewa, or Ojibway, called them *Nadowe-is-iw,* which signified "snakes" or "adders," and, by metaphor, "enemies." To the early French *voyageurs* and missionaries, pushing into the unexplored wilderness west of the Great Lakes, *Nadowe-is-iw* sounded like *Nadowessioux.* Soon thereafter the abbreviation *Sioux* was universally adopted, and it survived not only as the historical name of a very old and widely scattered people but also as the name of the tongue they spoke. As for their distribution, more than fifty Siouan tribes are known to have been inhabitants at some time of areas that are within the present boundaries of twenty-six states and three Canadian provinces.

Distinguished scholars estimate that when Columbus made his first New World landfall between a million and a million and a half Indians were living in the territory below Canada that eventually would be divided among forty-eight American states. As the Siouan linguistic family was surpassed in size in North America only by the Algonquian, it seems probable that in prehistoric times the Siouan population was the largest in the United States region, for a major part of the Algonquian people always dwelt north of the present Canadian border.

At the time of their discovery—in the third decade of the seventeenth century—the western Sioux called themselves *Óciti Sakowin,* meaning the "seven council fires," an appellation that apparently did not impress itself upon French minds, for it was not used by early explorers and priests. If the subdivisions of the Siouan linguistic family inhabiting the American Southeast in the colonial period possessed a general name, it was not preserved.

For an unknown number of millennia before any Europeans met them in their historical homelands, either in the East or in the Midwest, the Sioux were Indians of the woodlands, the prairies, hills, mountains and river valleys, that stretched in a continuous, luxuriant wilderness from the middle Mississippi River to the southeastern Atlantic Coast.

Therefore, it becomes obvious that at an even earlier time they must have passed through extreme northern parts of North America— Alaska and western Canada—for, like all Indians, they were emigrants from Asia.

Yet there is no evidence to suggest when the Sioux (or, for that matter, any other American Indian people) reached the Western Hemisphere by crossing the Bering Strait from Siberia. There is nothing to indicate how many years, or centuries, they may have spent in their southward migration. Nor is it possible to depict with any degree of accuracy the route they followed.

There are, however, some good reasons for believing that the Sioux were among the oldest inhabitants of the main United States region. For example, grinding tools similar to those of the Cochise culture, which arose more than sixteen thousand years ago in the American Southwest, have been recovered from archaeological sites in central states of this country and are thought to be of Siouan origin. There have been found, as well, in association with Siouan artifacts in this same midland region, stone spear points and scrapers much like those of the Folsom Culture that prevailed on the high western plains thirteen thousand years before the beginning of the Christian Era.

Thus, it appears quite possible that blood relatives of the Sioux living today were in American territory coincident with, if not previous to, the development of such ancient cultures. If, for lack of incontrovertible proof, that contention must remain in the realm of conjecture, at least it can be stated without fear of contradiction that people from Asia, whatever may have been their identity, had filtered far southward into the continent of North America before the Pleistocene, or Ice Age, had come to an end some twenty-five thousand years ago.

Perhaps in the future, scientists may solve some of the mysteries surrounding the genesis of the Sioux. The hands of the anthropological clock are steadily being turned back. As things now stand, however, all that may be said is that the Sioux trail is very long, and its beginning is lost in the darkness of the unopened—and perhaps impenetrable—vaults of time.

This is a book about that trail when it first emerges from the haze of antiquity into light provided by Indian traditions, archaeological discoveries and early historical records.

John Upton Terrell

Siouan Tribes of Early Historic Times

DAKOTA DIVISION

TETON BRANCH:

Oglala   Oohenonpa
Sicángu (Brulé)   Itazipco (Sans Arcs)
Hunkpapa   Sihasapa
Miniconjou

SANTEE BRANCH:

Mdewkanton   Wahpekute
Wahpeton   Sisseton

YANKTON:

Yankton

YANKTONAI BRANCH:—

Yanktonai   Assiniboin
Hunkpatina

NOTE: The name *Dakota* comes from the Santee dialect. In the Teton dialect it is *Lakota*, and in the Yankton and Yanktonai dialects it is *Nakota*. In all forms it signifies *allies*.

CHIWERE DIVISION

Winnebago	Hidatsa
Mandan	Crow
Iowa	Missouri
Oto	

DHEGIHA DIVISION

Omaha	Osage
Ponca	Kansa
Quapaw	

TRIBES WHOSE CONNECTIONS WITH DIVISIONS ARE UNCERTAIN

Moneton	Manahoac
Monacan	Nahyssan
Occaneechi	Saponi
Tutelo	Keyauwee
Woccon	Yadkin
Cape Fear	Catawba
Congaree	Pedee
Santee	Sewee
Waxhaw	Waccamaw
Cheraw	Eno
Shakori	Sissipahaw
Sugaree	Wateree
Winyaw	Biloxi
Mosopelea (Ofo)	Pascagoula
Moctobi	

NOTE: The Pascagoula are thought to be of mixed Muskhogean and Siouan blood. The Moctobi may have been a part of the Biloxi, or Moctobi may have been a Biloxi name for the Pascagoula.

PART ONE

The Oldest Trail

1

The Sioux were in their first identifiable homeland—composed of parts of Ohio, Kentucky, Indiana, Illinois and perhaps Tennessee—in the stage which archaeologists call Archaic, and which began about ten thousand years ago. It was a time when animals of the Pleistocene, such as the mammoth, the sloth, the giant bison and other Ice Age species were still hunted, although their numbers were rapidly diminishing and they would soon become extinct.

It was an incredibly bountiful land, indeed, an Indian paradise. A network of rivers, large and small, contained an abundance of fish and shellfish—mussels or clams. Forests of oak, hickory, yellow poplar, ash, maple, black walnut, white elm, beech, linden, locust, willow and sycamore blanketed the gentle hills and valleys. Wild fowl, ducks, geese, pigeons, in countless millions darkened the sky. In the woodlands and marshes and prairie meadows lived an endless variety of game, valuable for both meat and pelts—buffalo, deer, antelope, elk, bear, panther, wolf, fox, rabbit, muskrat, raccoon, opossum and many other types. Wild foods, fruits, berries, nuts, abounded in seasonal profusion. Except for brief periods in winter and midsummer, the climate was moderate, usually half of each year being free of frost.

The culture of the Archaic-period Siouans is called Indian Knoll. The name Indian Knoll was selected with good reason. The knolls were not natural elevations. They were created by the discarded shells of mussels which the Indians had consumed.

These shell mounds were located along the river shoals, where the mussels were most abundant. The villages of the people stood on them. Their shelters were crude, made of interwoven saplings and covered with skins. The shells, as well as the bones of animals and birds, were thrown about the campsites and cooking fires. Apparently, as the refuse mounted about them, the Indians moved their fragile dwellings a few feet or a few yards to prevent their view of the surrounding areas from being obscured. This is indicated by the size of the shell mounds. Some of those discovered were spread over from three to seventeen acres, and ranged in height from four to twelve feet. Obviously, there is no way of determining how many years were required to create mounds of such great dimensions. All that can be said is that it took an inconceivable number of shells and a very long time.

If archaeologists had been obliged to depend entirely on information gained from shell mounds, knowledge of the way of life of the Indian Knoll people would be extremely limited. Grave sites have been found in them, but the only artifacts recovered were such common things as stone manos used for grinding wild foods, spear points, scrapers and knives made of chipped stone, grooved stone axes and hammerheads, all attributes of most Archaic-period cultures. Fortunately, Indian Knoll Siouans also lived in hillside rock shelters and caves. In these protected dwelling places have been preserved a variety of articles fashioned from materials that would have disintegrated under long exposure to the elements, among them tools and utensils made of wood and horn—wooden spear-throwers or atlatls, clothing, baskets, and bone fishhooks, tubes, perforators and awls.

When bows and arrows reached the region of the United States is a question for which there is no possible answer. Eskimos may have possessed them as early as 1000 B.C. Scientists believe, however, that they were not widely used by American Indians until relatively late in prehistoric times. It is known that people of the Anasazi culture of the Southwest used them after A.D. 500, but there is no dependable evidence to show when they came into general use in the Midwest. The most that can be said is that arrow points found in archaeological sites of the Illinois and Ohio areas have been attributed to cultures existing after A.D. 700.

Indian Knoll people wore breechclouts, moccasins, robes and shirts (possibly with sleeves) woven from fibers and feathers or made from dressed skins. Their ornaments illustrate a lack of aesthetic development. They decorated their garments with snail shells, and adorned themselves with necklaces of bone and stone beads, pendants of perforated animal teeth, and bone pins.

The dead were interred in circular pits, usually in a flexed position. That they held dogs in high esteem is indicated by the custom of sacrificing them and placing them in the graves of their masters.

Sometimes turtles were buried with children, but whether this practice was connected with religious ritual is not known.

Skeletal remains unearthed by anthropologists denote the general physical characteristics of the Indian Knoll Siouans. They were people of medium stature, sturdy and muscular. Their heads were rather high vaulted, their faces short, their noses of medium width. It is not believed that very many Archaic Indians of the eastern and central woodlands lived very long lives. Witthoft asserts that the "Indian of the forest seldom lived to his fortieth birthday, usually dying before he was thirty-five." Life was rigorous and perilous in the extreme. Infections, especially those caused by diseased teeth, exposure and hunting accidents contributed to an early death.

Martin expresses the opinion that the Indian Knoll Culture "probably was the end product of a long tradition of hunting, fishing and food-gathering," and notes that there is some suggestion of a relationship to the Folsom Culture [13,000 to 8000 B.C.]. Emphasis should be placed on this postulation. The most important Folsom archaeological sites discovered are in Colorado and New Mexico, although Folsom material has been found, as Martin writes, scattered throughout most of North America *east of the Rocky Mountains.* But, except for a few examples of this culture found in California, *none has been located west of the Rockies.* The words I have emphasized do not justify any conclusions, but in my mind certain questions are insuppressible. Did the Indian Knoll Siouans come south through Montana, Wyoming and Colorado before turning eastward? Were they nomadic hunters on the high short-grass plains east of the Rocky Mountains in the period of the Folsom Culture?

Conclusive evidence can be proffered regarding their comparatively short migrations in midland America. There the center of the territory occupied by them seems to have been on Green River in Kentucky. Of particular interest, as Hyde remarks, is the fact that these Archaic Siouans of Kentucky comprise "the earliest Indian group whose movements can be followed with any degree of certainty. They migrated slowly toward the south, southwest, north, northeast, northwest and, perhaps, the west, taking their type of crude culture with them. To the historians, this situation strongly suggests that these Indians were a homogeneous stock, speaking one language, and that as their population increased, they spread in every direction from their old central area."

The courses of most of the migrations of the Indian Knoll people are delineated by rivers—the Ohio, Tennessee, Kentucky, Green, Mississippi, Illinois, Wabash and many lesser streams. But there were also important expansions eastward, out of the midland valleys, over ranges of the Allegheny Mountains and into watersheds of the Atlantic seaboard.

It is not possible to construct a chronological schedule of the movements. They took place over many years of the Archaic and later cultural periods, both before and after the Siouans had acquired pottery and tobacco pipes and knowledge of farming, innovations that marked significant transitions in their way of life and influenced the distribution of their population.

The spreading of the Indian Knoll Culture, however, is traceable in nine states:

Kentucky: Throughout most of the northern part, on the Mississippi River in the west, along the Ohio River from its mouth to the falls (Louisville) and eastward to the area of Campbell and Bracken counties.

Tennessee: Along the Tennessee River and its tributaries, in Henry, Stewart, Houston and adjacent counties, and in the eastern part of the state.

Alabama: In the northern part, along the Tennessee River and other streams, in the Pickwick, Wheeler and Wilson basins.

North Carolina, South Carolina and Virginia: Along streams of the Piedmont Plateau.

Ohio: Along the Ohio River, in the Cincinnati area and eastward to Adams County.

Indiana: Along the Ohio River, at the falls (opposite Louisville, Kentucky), in Dubois County, on streams entering the Ohio River from the north, on the Wabash River and in Dearborn and Franklin counties and the adjacent area.

Illinois: Along the Ohio and other rivers in the southern part, in Jackson County, on the Illinois River in Fulton County.

Most of the migrations to Ohio, Indiana, Illinois, Tennessee and Alabama are believed to have taken place before the Siouans possessed pottery, but the movements over the eastern mountains to the Piedmont Plateau definitely appear to have been undertaken after they had learned to make crude clay utensils, had adopted pipes as a part of their ritual and cultivated fields of corn, beans, tobacco and other crops.

How early Siouan people became established in Wisconsin and

Minnesota may not be stated with any degree of accuracy. It is not believed they invaded these northern woodlands until sometime after the beginning of the Christian Era. It is certain, however, that they had occupied this region by A.D. 700, for a culture called Effigy Mound, unquestionably of Siouan origin, began to appear there about this time.

2 Pod corn, the wild ancestor of maize, is a native of Central America and northern South America. It was first domesticated in these tropical regions by Indians. Each seed of wild pod is enclosed in a husk, and the plant reseeds itself. By crossbreeding and cultivation of pod corn and its "cousins," these early Indian farmers developed a corn much better and easier to use. It was incapable of reseeding itself and, like the corn of today, would not survive unless replanted and tended by man, but it had many advantages. It was easy to harvest, produced cobs bearing numerous kernels, and it could be preserved and transported.

Through migrations, the spreading of cultures and over trading routes, maize was steadily distributed until it had become the most important and widespread cultivated food plant in the entire New World. The oldest maize so far discovered, according to Driver, "is that from southern Puebla, Mexico, which has been dated at about 5000 B.C." How rapidly did it spread northward to the region of the United States? That cannot be determined for all areas of this country, but a partial answer is found in the story of Bat Cave, New Mexico.

Excavating in this large rock shelter in 1948, two noted botanists, Paul S. Mangelsdorf and C. Earle Smith, Jr., came upon ears of primitive maize. Laboratory analysis revealed that this Indian corn was a variety grown in Mexico at least as early as 4000 B.C. It was both a pod corn and a popcorn. The ears were not enclosed in husks. On later levels of Bat Cave a much newer type of maize was found. The cobs and kernels were larger, and it had a husk similar to modern corn. It was given a date of about A.D. 1. Here was evidence of long crossbreeding to improve yield.

No discovery comparable in antiquity to the oldest Bat Cave corn has been made in the area occupied by the Indian Knoll Siouans. However, other people inhabiting regions directly to the south of them are known to have cultivated maize and other crops approximately three thousand years ago, and it is not improbable that they grew these invaluable foods before that time.

Beans (many varieties) were the second most important plant food, and the squashes ranked third. Both beans and squashes were first domesticated either in Mexico or Central America. Domesticated beans six thousand years old have been found in the Ocampo Caves of Tamaulipas, Mexico. The domestication of squashes may have been achieved at a much earlier date, for remains of the *pepo* species nine thousand years old have been recovered in the same caves. Beans and squashes probably reached the American midland as early as maize, but proof is lacking. It can be definitely stated, however, that in southern Kentucky some Indians depended upon these three foods for at least half of their subsistence more than three thousand years ago.

Nothing is more American than tobacco, pipes and cigars. In every Indian language there are words meaning tobacco plant. Some forty varieties have been classified. The most widely used species originated in South America, but some varieties are native to western North America. The Indian Knoll Siouans are not known to have used tobacco. It reached midland America from Mexico. In innumerable localities archaeologists have discovered that pipes appeared about the same time as maize.

The first pottery known to have reached the area of the continental United States was found at Stallings Island, on the coast of Georgia. It was similar in some traits to ceramics which have been discovered in western South America. Scientific analysis indicated that it was approximately 4700 years old.

Prehistoric South American and Caribbean Indians made long trading voyages, and could easily have reached the mainland of the southern United States. Evidently their pottery did reach it, if not on direct voyages then by transfer from people to people along the way. The distribution of pottery also occurred over land routes running north from Mexico into the southwestern United States. From this area it spread slowly eastward.

When the art of molding and firing vessels of clay developed in the Midwestern region must remain a matter of conjecture. Indians there probably knew that ceramics existed long before they were able to manufacture them. According to Josephy, about 2000 B.C. undecorated fiber-tempered pottery appeared on the Tennessee River in northern Alabama. Undoubtedly it came into the area from the southeastern coast or the Gulf of Mexico coast. This part of the Tennessee River was on the perimeter of territory occupied by early Siouans, but pottery has not been discovered in the early sites of the Indian Knoll Culture.

3   About the time of the advent of the Christian Era, give or
     take a few centuries, a great cultural revolution had its
     beginning in midland America. Northward from the south-
     ern forests came Indians whose physical characteristics
     were in sharp contrast to the Indian Knoll people. They were
     small folk, very few of whom attained more than medium
     height. They had long faces, and they practiced head defor-
     mation, flattening the soft skulls of infants by binding them
     tightly to cradleboards.

     These southern Indians not only imposed their own cul-
     ture, called Adena,* on the Siouans of the Midwest but
     brought with them many of the basic elements of the
     Hopewell Culture, which, in ensuing years, represented the
     richest and most advanced Indian civilization to arise in
     prehistoric times north of Mexico.

     It was not an aggression, not a martial invasion, but a
     peaceable infiltration, the cause of which remains obscure.
     The Adena possessed wondrous things, such as seeds to
     plant, attractive ornaments, pottery utensils, effigy tobacco
     pipes and, most fascinating of all to the Indian Knoll people,
     religious beliefs and ritual that were stimulating, colorful
     and inspiring. They worshiped spirits, or gods, whom they
     believed dwelt in heavenly realms, and this doctrine drasti-
     cally transformed the traditional faith of the Siouans, who
     previously had revered only earthbound animal gods.

     Nothing has been discovered to indicate that the Siouans
     attempted to stop the northward migration of the Adena
     people or unwillingly granted them territorial rights. How-
     ever, Hyde asserts that there were "conservative groups
     even in those far-off times, and part of the tribes clung to old
     ways, shunned the new gods, and regarded with abhorrence
     the wicked new custom of wounding Mother Earth's skin

     ---

     *The name of an estate near Chillicothe, Ohio, on which the first important
     type-site was excavated by archaeologists.

with hoes made of flint or shell, thrusting alien seeds into her flesh to force her to produce hitherto unheard-of crops." Undoubtedly that was true, but the protests, probably voiced by a very small segment of the Siouan population, in no way disrupted the diffusion of the Adena Culture. It spread steadily from northern Alabama, where it first appeared in Siouan territory, into Tennessee, Kentucky, southern Ohio and West Virginia.

The Adena were the first Indians of North America to construct immense burial mounds. The great size of these works, built of earth, rock and timber, is proof of the existence of a social structure capable of organizing and maintaining cooperative labor projects on a large scale. Martin states it is "also possible that the Adena culture contained the seeds of city-state confederacy, a style of government found in later cultures in the Mississippi Valley." The Siouans had soon abandoned their custom of interring the dead in shell middens and the floors of caves and had adopted the elaborate Adena burial practices. Moreover, the Siouans themselves, in time, would extend the custom of building burial mounds, many of them in the form of animals, birds and reptiles, to Wisconsin, Minnesota and Iowa.

Hundreds of Adena burial mounds are known to have existed, but a great many of them were leveled and destroyed by farmers before scientists could excavate them. In most mounds there were usually a large central tomb lined with logs. In these mausoleums important personages, perhaps chiefs, highly honored warriors and revered spiritual leaders, were buried. In the mounds also were clay cremation basins, and archaeologists think that it was a common practice to cremate rank-and-file people.

Funeral ceremonies were carried out with great care, and were complex and marked with ornateness. Copper, mica and stone jewelry and ornaments were interred with the bodies of prominent persons. Adena burial mounds ranged in height from ten to seventy feet. Around some of them were earthen walls constructed in circles, rectangles and ovals. In several places these walls also enclosed what were apparently ceremonial centers in which the Indians gathered periodically to honor the dead. Notable ceremonial centers have been discovered near Chillicothe, Miamisburg and Cincinnati in Ohio, in southeastern Indiana and in the Kanawha Valley of West Virginia.

The villages of the Adena were small but their houses were large. Four or five houses usually stood close to each other, with similar groups adjacent, so that in effect a large area was settled. The houses were round, with diameters of thirty to fifty feet. The walls were built of saplings placed in the ground in pairs and slanted outward, providing greater width at the eaves than at floor level. Willow switches were woven among the saplings. Roofs were peaked and covered with bark. Some structures with diameters twice as great as the ordinary house are believed to have been community centers or the dwellings of chiefs.

That the trading relationships of the Adena were widespread is evidenced by their use of mica, which came from North Carolina, copper from the Lake Superior area and conch and other species of shells from the Gulf of Mexico.

But this commerce in which the Adena obviously were engaged is not as unique as it may seem at first thought. There is indisputable proof that far back in prehistoric times—no one may say how far—a network of Indian trade trails reached from ocean to ocean and from the tropics to the Arctic wastes.

Trade influenced the development of Siouan cultures in the Midwest, in the Southeast, in the Northern prairies no less than it did the cultures of other peoples. Indeed, for all Indians there could have been few vital changes—either social, intellectual or economic—without a steadily increasing diffusion of ideas, customs and products through a constantly enlarging primitive commerce. Trade spread knowledge and awakened minds. It gave one man the opportunity to learn from another. Trade distributed materials—animal, vegetable and mineral in raw form and as manufactured goods—to raise standards of living, to increase comfort and to improve health. The prehistoric Indian's intellect was limited by his way of life and his environment, not by his mental capacities. He was eager to learn and to improve himself. And there were two ways in which he could accomplish these things—by observation and by social intercourse.

The economy of the American wilderness cannot justifiably be termed simple. It was simple only in the sense that it was founded on barter. There were too many products and too many varieties of them, and they represented too many cultures, and they were transported over distances too great, to permit usage of the words *a simple economy.* In midland America the main arteries of commerce followed the courses of rivers and smaller streams. From the Archaic period until long after white men had encountered them, the Siouans dwelt in various regions adjoining the greatest of all trade-route networks—the Mississippi and its countless tributaries.

4

The progress of Indian cultures in the Ohio Valley and adjacent areas is clearly traceable through three main stages, the last of which endured almost to the beginning of the historical period.

In the Paleo-Indian stage there were nomadic groups who lived entirely by hunting and gathering wild plant foods. They wandered ceaselessly through the vast wilderness in an eternal search for game and to take advantage of the seasonal crops of nuts, berries and roots. Their linguistic relationships are unknown.

In the following Archaic stage, tribes of Siouans occupied various parts of this Midwestern region. They also were hunters and wild-plant-food gatherers, but they depended on shellfish for a large part of their sustenance. Due to the great supply of clams in the river shoals they were able to live a sedentary life, establishing their villages on shell mounds. Their culture became known as Indian Knoll.

Then came the Adena from the South. Now there was not only a blending of cultures but a mingling of peoples of contrasting physical types, of Northern Sylvids and Southern Centralids.* The Sioux, who were Sylvids, greatly outnumbered the Southerners and, although they adopted the main traits of the Adena Culture, they never relinquished their political or military supremacy. And in time, as a result of their innate skill as organizers and their unwavering dedication to the forms of ritual to which they had turned, they acquired spiritual dominance. Under their leadership, from the basic elements of the Adena culture, evolved the remarkably elaborate and complex culture to which scientists would give the name Hopewell.†

---

*The heads of people called Sylvids were long, with high vaults, and their faces were relatively narrow. Centralids had round heads, vaults of medium height and broad faces.
†Named for the owner of an Ohio farm on which many of its finest treasures were unearthed.

The Hopewellians carried the Adena religious ceremonialism, the cult of the dead and mound building to their highest levels. To these achievements they added artistry, craftsmanship and material and economic developments unprecedented in prehistoric times within the present boundaries of the United States.

The influences of the Ohio Hopewell Culture, spreading with remarkable rapidity among peoples of other regions, were both stronger and more widely diffused than those of any other American Indian culture. Hopewell centers have been discovered in Michigan, Pennsylvania, New York, Tennessee, Indiana, Illinois, Iowa, Kansas and on the lower Mississippi River.

A major force giving impetus to the swift rise and the spreading of the Hopewell Culture was generated by the establishment of fairly dependable and extensive trade channels. The Hopewellians were not only instigators in the development of these routes but they also encouraged visits of traders from other Indians, and they sent their own traders on round-trip journeys of hundreds and even thousands of miles to obtain articles. Their primary purpose was to secure both raw materials and manufactured goods to place with the dead in the immense burial mounds. Religious beliefs and ceremonials, therefore, stimulated the economy in many parts of the country and effectively diffused Hopewellian traits and products. A notable example is the remarkable Marksville culture of the Florida Keys, which strongly reflected Hopewell influences.

To the Hopewell people from the Gulf of Mexico region, either carried by their own traveling salesmen or by traders from other Indians, were brought conch shells, alligator teeth, pottery, sharkskins and sharks' teeth and the beautiful plumes and feathers of semitropical fowls. From the region bordering the Atlantic were brought mica, shells, wampum beads and various types of chert. From the upper Mississippi Valley and the Lake Superior region were brought lead and copper. From the Rocky Mountains were brought grizzly bear teeth and obsidian, both of which were highly prized.

Invariably Hopewell towns and ceremonial centers were located on the banks of streams and were enclosed by intricate systems of earthen walls, constructed in the forms of circles, squares and octagons. In numerous places the earthworks were hundreds of feet in length, and some extended along a river for more than a mile. These were not defense works, for they contained wide openings and some of the most extensive were no more than two or three feet in height. The walls,

within which stood the houses—probably made of saplings and bark—
the great earthen burial mounds, and the ceremonial centers, definitely had a religious function.

Three examples provide an understanding of the variety, complexity
and size of the earthworks and mounds. Among the most celebrated of
the effigy mounds is the so-called Great Serpent, which twisted for
more than thirteen hundred feet behind a wall on Brush Creek, in
Adams County, Ohio. At the head of the serpent was a large oval
enclosure, and the tail wound in circles.

A different type was located on the east bank of the Little Miami
River in Hamilton County, Ohio. The oval enclosure was fifteen
hundred feet long, and the surrounding wall was only two feet in
height but twenty feet wide at its base. At one end of the great oval
was a gateway. At the other end a graded road six hundred feet in
length led to an elevated circular mound with a diameter of five
hundred feet. Burial mounds built at various places within the
enclosure were also surrounded by walls.

On Raccoon Creek in Licking County, Ohio, stood one of the most
elaborate and complicated of all known earthworks. They were built
on a level area rising thirty to fifty feet above the bottomlands
bordering the stream. Spread over nearly four square miles, they
included a series of square, circular and octagonal enclosures, numerous mounds and other structures, all connected with avenues. Moats
ran along the interior side of an extensive network of embankments.
Unfortunately, as in the case of so many other Hopewell sites, many of
the Raccoon Creek mounds were leveled and the invaluable artifacts
they contained were destroyed or scattered by white settlers preparing
cornfields before archaeological investigations were conducted.

A large part of the Hopewell manufactured products had a sacred
function. They made excellent decorated pottery for ceremonial use.
No Indian people buried their dead with greater care and ceremony,
nor with more lavish contributions of burial offerings. Some graves
were lined with sheets of mica, with stones or with finely woven mats.
Beside the bodies were placed exquisitely carved bone, wood and metal
figures and scrolls, mosaics made of mineral paints, and necklaces,
beads, pendants, earrings and other ornaments of metal, shell and
bone. Oddly, some of the skeletons recovered bore bone lesions suggesting the presence of syphilis. If it was actually present, no earlier
appearance of the disease in the United States region is known.

The Hopewellians were the finest metalworkers of all prehistoric

Indians, and they made their magnificent ornaments, decorations, jewelry, headpieces and breastplates long before casting was known to any people of the Western Hemisphere. By beating and annealing, and with the aid of delicate tools they invented, they produced an incredible variety of articles out of copper and meteoric iron. Occasionally they used silver and gold in small amounts, but where they obtained these precious ores is not known.

But for all their ceremonialism, their concern for departed souls, and their incomparable artistry, the Hopewellians were a practical people, and the welfare and happiness of the living were of great importance to them. They made beautiful things to please the eye and satisfy the ego. They garbed themselves in fine furs and robes, well-tanned skins and woven cloth. They decorated themselves with copper, mica, shell, bone and wood ornaments. Both men and women wore copper and silver earspools and necklaces of freshwater pearls and animal teeth and bone beads. They were good hunters and fishermen. They were energetic and competent farmers, growing beans, maize, squash. And they were daring adventurers and courageous warriors.

The author wrote of them in *American Indian Almanac* that they

> had a highly developed social structure. Their projects and activities were well-planned and directed by able leaders who were probably members of an elite class. They had special guilds composed of metal workers, carvers, woodworkers, and traders—the first craft unions of America. Obviously they were ingenious organizers. Their society was divided into classes, yet it is not known that social cleavages disrupted their progress. Their earthworks and mounds were built by community labor, and all of them, regardless of rank and position, were imbued with ideals and desires that contributed to common advancement and affluence.
>
> They were bound together in what might be termed a loose confederacy, but not all of its segments followed precisely similar patterns. On the contrary, in each region customs and ceremonials were modified by local traditions and practices. No evidence has been found to indicate that the Hopewellians of Ohio, the center of the culture, attempted to force others to accept without deviation their mores and beliefs and ritual. It was a free society.

Archaeologists set the terminal date of the Hopewell Culture at approximately A.D. 1300. In some areas its influences survived perhaps as long as a hundred years after the end of the fourteenth century. It probably reached its zenith, however, between A.D. 1100 and A.D. 1200. It descended with more rapidity than it had ascended. What brought about its rather abrupt end was an amalgamation of different pressures. The growing number and the ferocity of intertribal wars brought about the collapse of the far-reaching network of trade routes. Other cultures were intrusive, reaching Hopewell regions especially from the south and west, and strong forces of aggressors and plunderers struck and maintained barriers. The most remarkable prehistoric Indian civilization that ever existed north of Mexico finally vanished forever from the sites on which it had risen.

A seemingly reasonable postulation is that before the beginning of the historical period—that is, the voyages of Columbus—most Siouan groups were gone from the Ohio Valley and its environs.

Unfortunately, scholars have found no means of determining with any degree of accuracy when any of the various tribes moved north and west from their ancient Midwestern homelands. Tribal traditions, while interesting and sometimes enlightening, are not acceptable as scientific evidence.

In regard to the eastern movements of the Sioux, however, a time sequence is indicated by credible information derived from archaeological discoveries.

PART TWO

The Eastern Sioux

". . . for when you ask them whence their Fore Fathers came, that first inhabited the Country, they will point to the Westward, and say, *Where the Sun sleeps our Forefathers came thence.* . . . And, to this day, they are a shifting, wandering People . . ."

John Lawson,
South Carolina,
1701

1 Indian Knoll Siouans had moved south from central Kentucky into Tennessee and northern Alabama before they used tobacco or possessed any form of ceramics. When some of them pushed on through eastern Tennessee and over the mountains to the North Carolina Piedmont they had learned to make a type of unpainted pottery and they smoked pipes. This archaeological intelligence suggests that an eastern movement may have begun as much as three thousand years ago, and possibly earlier, for as previously noted, pottery reached the Tennessee River Valley in northern Alabama about 2000 B.C. Eastward migrations continued, of course, from Kentucky, Ohio, and West Virginia, as well as from Tennessee, in later periods.

A North Carolina culture, called *Radin* by archaeologists, was similar in some respects to the much older Indian Knoll culture. Hyde states that Siouans "who remained in the upper Tennessee River Valley had a culture resembling the Radin Culture of North Carolina quite closely in some important features. Both groups lived in villages of circular huts, buried the dead flexed in round pit graves, used straight tubular stone pipes, and made crude grit-tempered pottery with fabric and cord marks on its surface."

The Siouans who migrated eastward over the mountains apparently were capable and well-organized warriors, for they drove out other Indians who occupied the Eastern region. Through the years they continued to spread out steadily, occupying strategic places on the many rivers that drained from the highlands through the coastal plain and into the ocean. They built strongly fortified towns, and cultivated maize, beans, squashes, tobacco and other plants, and they were skillful hunters of the great variety of game that existed in all parts of the Southeastern woodlands and marshes.

At last twenty-five Siouan tribes had established themselves in various advantageous locations between northern

Georgia and central Virginia. Some of the names by which these tribes eventually would be identified in recorded history are corruptions of some word in their respective dialects, but the origin and meaning of most tribal names are unknown.

2

The main Siouan tribes of the Southeast, and their first known homelands in historical times:

WEST VIRGINIA

MONETON: They lived for an indeterminate number of years on the Kanawha River, and then moved eastward into Virginia. Their name means "Big Water People," and Indian traders first heard it about 1671.

VIRGINIA

MANAHOAC: Their towns were in Spotsylvania, Stafford, Orange, Fauquier and Culpeper counties, and knowledge of the tribe was first recorded in 1608. The meaning of their name is not known.

MONACAN: When first heard of by white men, in 1607, they lived chiefly along the James River, above the falls at Richmond. While their name is believed to come from their own language, its meaning is uncertain.

NAHYSSAN: They lived on the James River in Nelson County, possibly early in the seventeenth century, and may have had other villages southwest of Petersburg. Their name apparently is a contraction of other Siouan names, and cannot be properly translated.

OCCANEECHI: The center of their territory was an island in the Roanoke River, near Clarksville, in Mecklenburg County. Colonists first heard of them about 1650, but an interpretation of their name has not survived.

SAPONI: This tribe was located on a map early in the seventeenth century in the present Albemarle County. One

of their earliest towns is thought to have stood on the
Rivanna River not far from Charlottesville. The name is a
corruption, but may signify "Shallow Water."

TUTELO: About the middle of the seventeenth century a town
of this tribe stood near Salem, but they may have lived at an
earlier period on the Big Sandy River, which at one time was
called the Tutelo. Neither the origin nor meaning of the
name is known.

NORTH CAROLINA

KEYAUWEE: Oddly, no record of this tribe dated earlier than
1701 is known to exist. At this time they were living in
Guilford County. The significance of their name is not
known.

WOCCON: First mentioned by a British traveler in 1701,
when they were living in Wayne County. It is thought they
were a subdivision of the Waccamaw tribe of South Carolina, and may have moved late in the seventeenth century.
No interpretation of their name has been preserved.

YADKIN: Scientists gave the name of this tribe to an early
culture of the Piedmont, but its significance is unknown.
They were living on the Yadkin River in 1674 when the first
known mention of them by white men was recorded.

CAPE FEAR INDIANS: These Siouan people, whose native
designation has never been discovered, are believed to have
been encountered in the Cape Fear area by sixteenth-
century voyagers. It was not until 1661, however, that they
appeared under this name in recorded history. They may
have been closely related to the Waccamaw, who dwelt to
the south of them along the Waccamaw River.

SOUTH CAROLINA

CATAWBA: Their main homeland at the beginning of historical times was in York and Lancaster counties, but Catawba
also lived in North Carolina and west of the Blue Ridge

Mountains in Tennessee. They were first encountered by Spanish explorers in 1566, but the significance of the name was not recorded by them or by later frontiersmen.

CONGAREE: Seventeenth-century accounts place them in the vicinity of Columbia. Their name is undoubtedly a Siouan word, but its meaning is unknown.

PEDEE: English settlers, probably in the 1670s, found them on the Pee Dee River, some distance inland from the coast. It is possible that Spaniards had encountered them a century earlier. Their name may mean *"something good"* or "capable."

SANTEE: The first white men known to have met these people were Spaniards. In the middle of the seventeenth century they were on the middle course of the river that still bears their name, and which is thought to mean "the river."

SEWEE: They dwelt on the lower Santee River and along the coast to the south, and there is linguistic evidence in Spanish accounts suggesting that they were occupants of this coastal region at least as early as 1500, if not some years earlier. Their name may signify "island."

WAXHAW: They were Piedmont people whom the Spanish reported living in the present Lancaster County about 1566. The meaning of their name is not known.

WACCAMAW: Some linguists suggest that this name appeared in very early Spanish records as *Guacaya.* If that is correct, they were living on the Waccamaw and Pee Dee rivers about 1500. Neither of these names is translatable into English.

CHERAW: This tribe is believed to have left the area of Pickens and Oconee counties in the first years of the sixteenth century, and reestablished their villages in North Carolina, where they were met by Spaniards in 1540. The meaning of their name, if it was ever recorded, has been lost.

ENO: They lived on the Enoree River in very early colonial times, but most likely they occupied this area many years before this period. Their name may mean "people disliked."

SHAKORI: There is a possibility that they lived on the coast, perhaps near the mouth of the Edisto River or in this vicinity, in the first years of the sixteenth century, and later, after Spanish slavers had captured a number of them, moved far inland and joined the Eno on the Enoree River. An Indian "province" called *Chicora* in early Spanish annals may have been a corruption of their name, the significance of which is not known.

SISSIPAHAW: These people, of which very little is known, probably were neighbors, if not allies, of the Shakori. They were mentioned in the account of a Spanish expedition in 1569, but the meaning of their name has not survived.

SUGAREE: They are not listed in early colonial records, but at the end of the seventeenth century they lived on Sugar Creek in York County. It has been determined, however, that they were closely related to the Catawba (q.v.). Their name may mean "people stingy."

WATEREE: In 1567, according to a Spanish account, they lived in the northwestern part of the state, but a hundred years later they were located on the river which bears their name, near the present town of Camden. It is thought that Wateree derived from the Catawba word *wateran,* meaning "to float on the water."

WINYAW: Some scholars have suggested that this tribe was called *Yenyohol* in Spanish records as early as 1521. If that is the case, they lived below Charleston on the coast. It has been established, however, that their villages were on Winyaw Bay and the Pee Dee River in the middle of the seventeenth century, but the meaning of their name is not known.

3   Similarities in names sometimes serve to dispel shadows obscuring historical facts. *Shakori* was the name of a Siouan tribe. Early in the sixteenth century a Spanish exploring expedition reported that it had visited an Indian province called *Chicora*. It is believed by some ethnologists and linguists that to Spanish ears *Shakori* sounded like *Chicora*. If they are correct—others disagree with them—then it is highly possible that a Sioux was the first Indian from the United States mainland to be exhibited before the Spanish Court.

There is no certainty as to where, in 1521, Lucas Vázques de Ayllón landed on the South Carolina coast. He may have put into a number of bays. In any case, he and his men responded to the friendly overtures of the Indians by carrying off seventy of them—with the crew taxing the capacity of their small ship—to be sold into slavery in Cuba.

Four years later Ayllón sent a slaving expedition that was even more successful to the same area. Meanwhile, obsessed with a dream of finding great treasures, Ayllón had returned to Spain in quest of a royal patent that would permit him to establish a colony on the southeastern coast. He took with him one of his captives, whom he had christened Francisco de Chicora.

Chicora, as he was popularly called, a Stone Age Indian until his capture, obviously was gifted with a remarkable mentality and an exceedingly vivid imagination. He not only furnished Spanish historians and geographers with considerable factual information about his country, but he captivated the Spanish Court with glowing fables of the splendors and riches to be found in it.

The land of Chicora, said Chicora, was inhabited by men with long hard tails like alligators. Gold and all manner of precious jewels littered the earth. All one had to do to become fabulously wealthy was to gather the treasures in baskets. He would be pleased to furnish the baskets.

This was probably the first occasion on which an American Indian engaged in a practice that would be used countless times in later years. It was that of fabricating tales of a kind they understood white explorers most wanted to hear. De Soto would be a victim of this shrewd tactic a few years later in the Southeastern region.

With the aid of Chicora, who wanted nothing so much as to go home, Ayllón got the patent he sought, and he sailed from Spain with a strong expedition of six vessels and five hundred colonists. The venture was a complete disaster. The Spaniards found no gold, no jewels, not even men with long hard tails, but only a forbidding wilderness with which they were unable to cope. In a few cabins thrown up near the mouth of a large river, perhaps the Pee Dee or the Savannah, Ayllón and his settlers rapidly succumbed to malnutrition and disease. In the spring of 1527, only a hundred and fifty persons were still alive, and these human wrecks, starving in a land of plenty, managed to sail to Haiti, leaving their leader in a Chicora grave.

The fate of Francisco de Chicora is not known, but it is believed that by this time, having had all they wanted of white men, the Shakori had fled far inland and had joined the Eno. Other expeditions soon appeared to carry on the lucrative slave trade Ayllón had started, and within a few years some of the smaller coastal tribes, notably those affiliated with the Muskhogean Cusabo, who lived in the southernmost part of South Carolina and northern Georgia, were all but wiped out.

4 The Eastern Sioux are described by a number of early white observers as possessing excellent physiques. The men generally stood above medium height, the women were usually somewhat shorter, but both sexes were very straight and equally well proportioned. The color of their eyes varied from obsidian black to dark hazel, the white part commonly being marbled with fine red streaks. The shade of their skins ranged from sorrel to tawny. Baldness was unknown to them. They took pride in caring for their long, thick, dark hair, keeping it well greased with bear fat, which they maintained not only nourished it but kept lice out of it. For certain festivities they mixed the bear fat with a red powder. To obtain the powder, they ground in a stone mano a scarlet root that was found only in the mountains to the west, and which, because of its scarcity, was a highly prized and very expensive article of trade.

The teeth of many mature persons were stained a dull yellow from smoking, a habit to which both men and women were addicted. It was believed that nature had intended nails to serve a utility purpose, and they were permitted to grow long until they broke off. Men kept their faces clean of hair by pulling it out. Natural deformities seldom occurred, and blindness was rare.

Lawson, an Englishman trained as a surveyor, who first went among the Sioux in 1701, remarked upon their inherent agility and the gracefulness of their movements. He was particularly struck by the comeliness of the women, whom he thought "as fine shaped Creatures (take them generally), as any in the Universe. They are of a tawny Complexion, their Eyes very brisk and amorous, their Smiles afford the finest Composure a Face can possess, their Hands are of the finest Make, with small, long Fingers, and as soft as their Cheeks, and their whole Bodies of a smooth Nature."

In hot weather almost no clothing was worn. Males covered their genitals with a brief loincloth, the head of the penis being encased in a kind of sack. The customary summer dress of females was a short apron of soft doeskin, divided into front and back parts. Cold weather garb consisted of furs and dressed skins. Girdles, sashes and garters were made of a cloth of woven opossum hair. At ceremonies and on other solemn occasions, chieftains and medicine doctors wore long coats of finely sewn and matched turkey feathers which had the beauty and texture of deep silk shag.

5   With one exception, tribal governments were almost pure democracies. Only the eastern Santee tribe is known to have been an autocracy, the "king" of which possessed supreme civil and judicial powers. Although in many bands chieftainships were hereditary, leadership not infrequently was bestowed on an individual by popular acclaim, perhaps in recognition of his inherent sagacity or as a result of extraordinary shrewdness and prowess displayed in warfare.

Most Siouan groups were affiliated with several others for mutual support or common action as belligerents, such as the so-called Monacan, Tutelo and Manahoac confederacies, but there was no permanent supreme governing body in any of these leagues. Every member tribe retained the power to act independently of the others.

Questions involving military action, peace negotiations, social, economic and other civil affairs, as well as criminal problems, were openly debated and decided at public meetings with the chieftain and his councillors, who were invariably prominent elders of a tribe. Customarily the sufferer of a felonious act was entitled to gain revenge in almost any manner he desired. This might take the form of harassment, social discrimination, cruelties inflicted on the offender, or the exaction of a sum of wampum (shell money) and quantities of beads, tobacco, skins and other goods. In a case of murder, close kin of the victim held the authority to follow this procedure, and generally did so, but it was also within their province, if they wished, to perform as both judge and executioner, and to retaliate by taking the life of the slayer of their relative. Thefts were not common among residents of a community or even among members of a tribe. While they were not viewed lightly, corporal punishment was not always inflicted on the offenders. If a man stole corn from the field of a neighbor, for example, he was sentenced to work for the person robbed at planting and cultivating another crop.

But a crime that endangered the public welfare, or which may have resulted in the deaths of persons in no way responsible for arousing the passions of the perpetrator, was a matter in which the entire tribe was called upon to take action as a juridical tribunal. Invariably capital punishment was ordered. Lawson tells of witnessing the sufferings and execution of a man found guilty of poisoning a village spring, presumably in retaliation for some action against him which he felt was an injustice. So heinous was this crime considered that even the culprit's relatives urged that he be put to death, and nothing would appease the villagers, some of whom had succumbed to the poisoned water and all of whose lives had been menaced,

> but the most cruel Torment imaginable . . . executed in the most publick Manner . . . the whole Nation, and all the Indians within a hundred Miles (if it is possible to send for them), are summoned to come and appear at such a Place and Time, to see and rejoice at the Torments and Death of such a Person, who is the common and professed Enemy to all the friendly Indians thereabouts, who now lies under the Condemnation of the whole Nation. . . . Then all appear (young and old), from all the adjacent Parts, and meet, with all the Expressions of Joy, to consummate this horrid and barbarous Feast, which, is carried on after this dismal Manner. First, they bring the prisoner to the Place appointed . . . where he is set down on his Breech on the Ground. Then they all get about him and you shall not see one sorrowful or dejected Countenance amongst them, but all very merrily disposed, as if some Comedy was to be acted instead of a Tragedy. He that is appointed to be the chief Executioner, takes a Knife and bids him hold out his Hands, which he does, and then cuts round the Wrist through the Skin, which is drawn off like a Glove . . . then they break his Joints and Bones, and buffet and torment him after a very inhuman Manner, till some violent Blow perhaps ends his Days; then they burn him to Ashes and throw them down the River. Afterwards they eat, drink and are merry, repeating all the actions of the Tormentors, and the Prisoner, with a great deal of Mirth and Satisfaction.

Lawson, however, does not trouble to mention that the manner in which the Siouan poisoner was put to death was no more barbaric than the fiendish tortures inflicted on condemned men in European prisons, including those of his own country, England, or the indescribable cruelties suffered by Indians at the hands of the Spanish conquistadors, with whose history he professed to be familiar.

6   The attitudes of the Eastern Sioux about sex were extremely
liberal. It was viewed simply as a natural bodily function, no
more subject to spiritual influences than eating, sleeping,
breathing and excretion. The few regulations and taboos
enforced were those practiced by most American Indians.
Mating between persons regarded as genetic relations,
either by consanguinity or tradition, was considered incest,
and was strictly forbidden. The social structures of some
tribes were even more extreme, and prohibited men and
women from marrying within their own clan or sib, despite
an absence of blood relationship. This exogamy might be
applied to an entire locality, in which case persons were
required to seek mates outside the village, or even beyond
larger defined areas, in which they made their homes.

Ostracism for life was probably the least penalty inflicted
on men and women guilty of incest. Women could be
branded professional prostitutes, considered unfit to be
married, and forbidden to participate in the affairs of their
people, but death by torture could be decreed for male
violators of the restriction by a tribal council, or in some
tribes by only a chief. Lawson unequivocably states that "if
a man lies with his Sister, or any very near Relation, his
Body is burnt, and his Ashes thrown into the River, as
unworthy to remain on Earth." He adds significantly that as
far as he was able to determine, the Siouan language
contained no word meaning sodomy, and insists that the
unnatural practice was not "heard of amongst them."

The noted anthropologist, Aleš Hrdlička, made the general statement that "the condition of the skeletal remains, the
testimony of early observers, and the present state of some
of the tribes in this regard, warrant the conclusion that on
the whole the Indian race was a comparatively healthy one."
Nothing has been found, either by scientific investigations
or in the oldest documents and accounts, to suggest that the
Eastern Sioux should not be included in this category both

before and at the time of contact with Europeans. While not a great deal is known of their endemic diseases, it is believed that they seldom if ever attained epidemic proportions, and certainly never to the degree of the terrible scourges that swept through other continents. Moreover, no reports mention hunchbacks or persons otherwise deformed, and very few blind men and women were seen. Incomplete infants were not permitted to live.

Such virulent afflictions as venereal diseases, smallpox, scarlet fever, rachitis and tuberculosis were gifts from white men, and they took a heavy toll in Indian lives. As skillfull and as successful as the Sioux medicine men were in treating bodily disorders and curing injuries, and as extensive as their pharmacopoeia was, especially the innumerable medicines derived from vegetal sources, they had small success in combatting the ravages of syphilis, gonorrhea and smallpox, although they achieved considerable progress in arresting tuberculosis and in curing fevers and other ills which came to them with the invaders from across the sea.

Marriage customs of the Eastern Sioux were complex and varied somewhat from tribe to tribe, but some formalities and practices were identical in all tribes. Secret marriages, for example, could not occur, for it was a common rule that every marriage must be made known at the time of its consummation to everyone in a community. Also, neither a young man nor a young woman was free to marry without consulting with the parents and elders of both families and obtaining their approval of the union. If objections were strong enough the ceremony could not be performed. Thus, family members held supreme authority in the matter of the selection of a husband or wife. It was not considered immoral or even a challenge to family jurisdiction, however, for a young woman to bestow her physical charms on a young man of her choice without marriage.

The degree of liberality with which the Eastern Sioux and some other peoples of the Southeast regarded sex is cited in Driver's statement that

> both young men and women were allowed premarital sexual experience, which was taken for granted and was nothing to be ashamed of or kept secret. The only restriction was that they should not violate the rules regarding incest, exogamy or adultery. It was even legitimate for unmarried young women to sell themselves for a price, subject to these same restrictions, and this was carefully distinguished from professional prostitution on the part

of adulteresses who had been cast off by offended husbands. Prostitutes were looked down on but were tolerated. Premarital pregnancies were fairly common, and the children were reared by the mother's family, extended family or sib as a matter of course. While the child was apparently always kept within its mother's sib, it might be adopted by some family other than the mother's; or, if the unwed mother preferred, she had a right to put her infant to death within one month after birth. There was little or no stigma attached to the mother or the offspring of a premarital sexual union.

Such information, of course, is derived from scientific analyses of historical sources, and while it is unquestionably reliable it is wont to be extremely conservative. Thoroughly capable ethnologists and archaeologists did not come upon the American scene until well after Indian cultures had been greatly transformed by the pressures of white civilization. As there were no accounts of Indian social mores written by Indians, their conclusions have been drawn with the greatest caution. John Lawson, Gentleman (as he signed himself), was not a scientist but he possessed an abiding interest in Indian culture, and he was a keen observer. Siouans murdered him, for no other reason than that he was a white man and therefore an enemy, but he left to posterity an invaluable record of their way of life. It was a work based almost entirely on what he saw with his own eyes and heard from their own lips nearly three decades before Carolina officially became a royal colony and, even more significantly, before the last vestiges of the Stone Age had vanished from the Southeastern woodlands.

Regarding the sexual habits and other social customs of the Eastern Sioux he wrote in part:

> The Girls, at twelve or thirteen Years of Age, as soon as Nature prompts them, freely bestow their Maidenheads on some Youth about the same Age, continuing her Favors on whom she most affects, changing her Mate very often, few or none of them being constant to one, till a greater Number of Years can make her capable of managing domestic Affairs . . . Multiplicity of Gallants never being a Stain to a Female's Reputation, or the least Hinderance of her Advancement; but the more Whorrish, the more Honorable, and they of all most coveted by those of the first Rank to make a Wife of.

Dissolution of a marriage was easily accomplished, for

at the least Dislike, the Man may turn her away, and take another; or if she disapproves of his Company, a Price is set upon her, and if the Man that seeks to get her, will pay the fine to her Husband, she becomes free from him; Likewise, some of their War Captains, and great Men, very often will retain three or four Girls at a time for their own Use. . . . The Husband is never so enraged as to put his Adulteress to Death; if she is caught in the Fact, the Rival becomes Debtor to the Cornuted Husband, in a certain Quantity of Trifles, valuable amongst them, which he pays as soon as discharged, and then all Animosity is laid aside betwixt the Husband and his wife's Gallant.

In some tribes a number of the prettiest "faces are set aside as trading girls; these are remarkable by their Hair, having a particular Tonsure by which they are known and distinguished from those engaged to Husbands. They are mercenary, and whoever makes Use of them, first hires them, the greatest Share of the Gain going to the King's Purse, who is the chief Bawd . . . and his own Cabin (very often) being the chiefest Brothel-House."* Many couples, however, ". . . live together for many Years, faithful to each other, admitting none to their Beds but such as they owned for their Wife or Husband, so continuing to their Life's end."

Polygamy was practiced, a man being allowed to have as many wives as he could support, but marriages were "no farther binding than the Men and Women agree Together. Either of them has Liberty to leave the other upon any frivolous Excuse they cane make."

Divorce, however, was burdened by certain complications and rules.

Whoever takes the Woman that was another Man's [wife] before, and bought by him, as they all are, must certainly pay to her former Husband whatsoever he gave for her. Nay, if she be a widow, and her Husband died in Debt, whosoever takes her to Wife pays all her Husband's Obligations . . . yet the Woman is not required to pay anything that was owing from her Husband, so long as she keeps Single. But if a Man courts her for a Night's Lodging and obtains it, the Creditors will make him pay her Husband's Debts, and he may, if he will, take her for his Money, or sell her to another for his Wife. I have seen several of these Bargains driven in a day, for you may see Men selling their Wives as Men do Horses in a Fair . . .

It was considered a breach of propriety and bad manners for a man to

*Lawson called chieftains "Kings," and their councillors "Lords."

boast "about their intrigues with the Women. If they do, none of the Girls value them ever after, or admit of their Company in their Beds. This proceeds not on the score of Reputation, for there is no such thing (on that account) known amongst them; and although we may reckon them the greatest Libertines and most extravagant in their Embraces, yet they retain and possess a Modesty that requires those Passions never to be divulged."

As matrilocal postnuptial residence means living with or near the bride's family, a man could not live matrilocally with two wives who were unrelated and hence from two different families. According to Driver, "he had to break the residence rule and set up an independent residence of his own." But if a man married two sisters—a very common occurrence—"they might share the same house . . ."

Theoretically, and in some instances literally, the rules of the Europeans regarding sex were stringent when compared with those of the Siouans, but the attitudes of the colonists were hypocritical in the extreme. They did not practice what they preached. The claim that Europeans were not inconstant was wholly false. Indeed, Lawson believed that "were the old World and the new one put onto a Pair of Scales (in point of constancy) it would be a hard Matter to discern which was the heavier."

7   The dwellings of the Siouans (as the colonists first saw them) were built of stout poles set in the ground. They were usually round, although some were oval, and the poles were bent toward the center and lashed together with elm strips or the long so-called Spanish moss that hung from trees. Bark covering was placed over the entire structure, except at the peak of the roof, where there was an opening through which smoke might escape. They were stout, and their round construction thwarted the pressures of gales that frequently swept through the country. The furnishings consisted chiefly of bedsteads, tables and benches usually woven of reeds. The entrances were covered with hides that could be lashed shut against storms. Many houses were large enough to accommodate several related families. The pallets were covered with mats and, in cold weather, with soft skins and furs. The struggle to eradicate fleas was without end, but otherwise houses were relatively sanitary—much more so than a good many of the cabins occupied by whites—and the loose dirt floors were kept free of decaying rubbish. In warm weather the people cooked and dwelt much of the time in airy arbors. It was their custom to perform their bodily functions at a distance from their homes or hunting campgrounds. Storage cribs were built of posts closely set together, seven or eight feet in height. These were covered with laths and then plastered both inside and out with clay. The roofs were made tight in the same manner. There was one very small door of wood which was tightly sealed with mud. Corn and other perishables were well preserved in these structures, the smallest insects being unable to penetrate them.

The Siouans not only thought of themselves as the rightful owners of the land they inhabited but they also thought of themselves as a part of that land, inextricably woven into its scheme and, actually, into the natural scheme of the entire universe as they conceived it. They were not simply pieces of bone and flesh, not simply possessors of certain faculties. They were those things, but they were also of the earth, the winds, stars, plants and grasses, the trees and the thunder and the sun and the rain and the lightning—everything that was born and lived and died in the eternal cycle of life. It was impossible for them to understand the white man's custom of practicing religion one day a week, for their spiritual beliefs were never absent from their thoughts. And as they considered the bounties of the earth to be benefits for which they should be thankful, it was equally impossible for them to understand why the white man was interested in a natural resource only to the extent that it could be exploited for personal gain. Land belonged not to the individual but to all the people of a tribe. Beyond their comprehension was the fact that the white man attached no spiritual significance to the good earth or any of its treasures, and as incomprehensible to them was the white man's pattern of taking, raping, destroying and then looking elsewhere for opportunities to repeat the process.

The Siouan paid obeisance to Supreme Beings, but he had no conception of a hereafter, such as the Christian Heaven and Hell. Their religion was a system of imitative and sympathetic magic aimed ritually at fulfillment of the requirements of life and living. It was not concerned with preparation for death and afterlife. Although like any sane human being, a Sioux attempted to prolong his life, he did not live in morbid fear of dying. Death was looked upon as the normal end of a life cycle for man, just as it was for plants and animals. When death came, a man or women became one with the cosmos, a condition that brought no punishment—water poured into a river was no longer identifiable in itself.

Missionaries were never able to induce the Siouans to accept the belief that there was only one God, who was all good. There were, they maintained—and this was true of most Indians—both good and bad spirits. The good spirit created everything beneficial, such as the fruits of the earth, and made it possible for them to hunt and fish, and to be wise enough to overpower the beasts that would destroy them. The bad spirit tormented them with sicknesses, disappointments, hunger and other misfortunes. They sought to appease both of these powerful supernaturals.

Detailed information on the ancient Siouan ceremonies, feasts and dances as white men first witnessed them is woefully lacking. Europeans were more interested in acquiring riches than in native religious ritual. Traders and colonists ridiculed them. Missionaries condemned them as idolatrous and sought to suppress them. By the time intelligent scholars reached the region, many of the tribes had been destroyed or driven out. Lawson made some notes, but they were generalizations, and they were adulterated by his own religious prejudices. He spoke of the rites as "cheats," and "absurdities," but he did pay tribute to the beauty of the chanting and marveled at the harmony of the choruses.

Fortunately, in his research on the Eastern Sioux during the first quarter of this century, the ethnologist Frank G. Speck of the University of Pennsylvania found that several of the ancient ceremonies of the Siouan Tutelo were still scrupulously performed. These rituals had been preserved through some two centuries. About 1753, driven from their old homeland in Virginia, the Tutelo had been adopted into the Cayuga Tribe of the Iroquois and had moved northward from Virginia to Canada.

"That the Tutelo were singers and ceremonialists of a high order," he wrote, "is shown by the esteem in which they are still held in the traditions of the Cayuga.

"Two major rituals; the Redressing Ceremony and the Four Nights Ceremony, and also one minor rite, the Bean Dance, are attributed to the Tutelo who brought them north." They are still contained in the Iroquois repertoire, are still performed, and are "definitely known to have been acquired from the Tutelo."

By virtue of this discovery, and Speck's fieldwork among the Cayuga, it is possible to describe these Siouan ceremonies largely as they existed in early colonial times, and probably long before the dawn of recorded history, at least among the Tutelo if not other tribes of the Eastern Sioux.

According to Speck,

> The Redressing Ceremony comes near to being the Tutelo national religious festival. It is performed when possible one year to the day after the death of a member of the Tutelo tribe, the purpose being to appoint a living representative of the same sex and approximate age to carry on the name and social functions of the deceased. At the same time it releases the soul of the deceased in whose behalf it is held from further durance on earth, from hovering near the earthly home as a ghost. It ushers the soul to the sky realm from the path opened heavenward on one of the rays of the sun rising at daybreak after the ceremony. The Redressing Ceremony lasts an entire night.
>
> Properly upon the death of each Tutelo another person is raised

up to receive and perpetuate his or her name. In this manner the identity of the deceased and the social consciousness of the Tutelo tribe are maintained and insured.

The Redressing Ceremony derives its name from the requirement that the family of the departed, the mourners, provide a new costume for the person chosen to receive the name of the deceased. [If it happened that several Tutelo had died during the year, one ceremony] . . . may then serve to create a number of living substitutes for the departed. [An attendant, or guide, from each mourning family] . . . is selected to remain at the side of the redressed person during the rite. Next in importance are the eight persons, six singers and a drummer and rattler, who throughout the night furnish the music for the solemn rite.

Speck recorded this prayer, which is offered by one of the men appointed to address the gathering:

> My relatives, I have the honor to represent the people now present in thanking the people for gathering at this time, Mother Earth, the animals, plants, food, fruits, maple trees (for sap), thunder, our grandmother the moon, our great brother the sun, our guardians the four angels [the winds] and particularly the Great Spirit who has created all.

It is estimated that one hundred and seventy songs were intoned during the night's performance. There was no dancing. The musicians were paid for their service in wampum beads.

Just before daylight, while a final chant is "being introduced by the musicians, the 'redressed' person and the performers go outside to await the first appearance of the sun's rays announcing the coming of a new day." As the first sunlight appears, "the soul of the deceased in whose behalf the ceremony is performed, which is thought to have returned for this night to be present in the rite among the mourning relatives, is believed to step on the sun's rays and depart to the sky."

The Four Nights Ceremony derives its name from the custom of being performed over four nights in four different homes. It is a ceremony of thanksgiving. At each of these places, says Speck, "the various fruits of the harvest have been gathered and piled in view of the thankful congregation. A feast for all those present is prepared, and in the morning what has not been consumed is distributed. Women only perform the dances while the men sit on a bench in the center and sing. They accompany themselves with the water-drum and the horn rattle . . . There are in all about eighty songs in the series to be repeated each of the four nights at each of the houses."

Both men and women take part in the Bean Dance, "each sex stepping in a single-file circular course around the singers. The men dancers represent beans and form the inside circle, the women in the outside circle represent corn. The movement of the dance represents the beans clinging to the corn while growing, in the picturesque imagery of the ancients. The horn rattle is the only instrument of accompaniment."

The four musical instruments used in the ceremonies are:

The water drum, made of fitted pieces of white oak covered with a skin. It contained a small quantity of water, which gave it a "ringing liquid tone."

The horn rattle contained pebbles, which were replaced with buckshot after the advent of guns.

Time beaters were made of basswood, about fourteen inches in length and one-quarter inch in thickness. They were used to strike measures, and were destroyed after each ceremony.

Garter rattles were attached to the legs of dancers. They consisted of a series of deer hoofs strung on leather, and produced "bell-like sounds."

The country of the Eastern Siouans abounded in countless varieties of game, large and small, fish, shellfish and fowl. Their diet was greatly varied and under normal conditions was well balanced. They hunted and fished, never killing animals for sport. While bear, deer, opossum, elk, ducks, geese and especially wild turkeys of which there were great flocks were preferred, cougars, rats, hares, wolves and squirrels were eaten. Certain parts of the viscera of large animals were considered tidbits. It was in all a land of great plenty, at least until after the arrival of the white traders. To the high-protein fare was added starches in numerous forms, such as wild potatoes, maize, beans, as well as a great number of wild foods such as berries, nuts and roots. Enormous sturgeons inhabited the rivers. A dinner particularly relished was an unborn fawn cut out of a doe's belly, and young wasps, white in their combs and unable to fly, were considered a dainty. Raccoons, opossums, hares, young wild cats and skunks were sometimes roasted without removing the entrails.

The Siouans were expert hunters and fishermen. They possessed great skill as bowmen. Sometimes they set fire to marshlands, driving the game out to enable them to kill animals with great ease. They used nets made of fibers to take large quantities of fish in the rivers and estuaries. Turkeys, ducks, geese, pelicans and other wild fowl were shot with arrows or snared.

Men normally planted the crops, although all persons, young and old, might take part in tending and protecting them from animals. The work of the women, however, was largely confined to the home, to cooking, weaving and caring for the children. The mats made by the women were woven of rushes, were five feet in width and as much as fourteen feet in length, ample in size for covering a double bed. Baskets were skillfully woven of both bullrushes and silkgrass, and were decorated with figures of animals, fishes and birds.

Their "money" was made from various types of hard shells found on the Carolina coast. Small pieces of the shells, which were very difficult to cut into the desired sizes, had holes drilled in them and were rubbed and polished until they were as smooth as glass. Some of these shell beads were of greater value than others. The customary measure of exchange was a string reaching from the elbow to the end of the little finger, and whether a man participating in the barter was tall or short was not a matter given consideration. Persons of affluence wore strings of the shell money draped about their necks.

The Eastern Sioux imposed extremely severe punishments on both boys and girls on the verge of reaching the age of puberty, it being their belief that such means not only held them in subjugation but forever hardened them to the fatigues they might expect to experience in adult life. The elders contended, moreover, that the prolonged ordeals disposed through death of many weak young people who, had they been permitted to grow, might well have turned out to be a burden and a disgrace to their tribe. Thereby, also, victuals and clothing were saved for stronger people that might otherwise have been wasted on useless creatures. There could be no doubt that youths who were able to endure the cruel practices and emerge with all their senses intact could very well withstand any hardships and frustrations that came their way.

Ethnologists state that, with the exception of the Algonquians, no other ceremonies of this extreme character have been reported anywhere else in Anglo-America east of the New Mexico Pueblos. According to these scientists, the Siouans had a special tribal initiation for adolescent girls, and the Algonquians of Virginia kept their males of ten to fifteen years of age in a specially constructed wilderness compound for nine months, not permitting them to speak with anyone during this entire period, although they were instructed in religious lore during their confinement.

Regarding the Siouan ceremonies of this type, an Englishman who lived among them in the first years of the eighteenth century wrote:

There is one most abominable custom amongst them, which they call *husquenawing* their young men . . . You must know that most commonly once a year, at farthest once in two years, these people undergo it, and *husquenaugh* them, which is to make them obedient and respectful to their superiors. They say it is the same to them as it is to us to send our children to school to be taught good breeding and letters. This house of correction is a large, strong cabin, made on purpose for the incarceration of the boys. It is always at Christmas that they *husquenaugh*, by taking them into this house and keep it dark all the time. They more than half starve them. Besides, they give them pellitory bark, and several intoxicating plants, that make them go raving mad, and you may hear them utter the most dismal and hellish cries and howlings . . . all of which continues about five or six weeks. The little meat they are given to eat is the nastiest, loathsome stuff, and mixed with all manner of filth. After the time of imprisonment is expired they are brought out of the cabin—which is never in a town, but always a distance off in the woods, and always guarded by jailors. When they first come out they are as poor as ever any creatures were. Several die under this diabolical purgation. Moreover, they really are, or pretend to be dumb, and do not speak for several days, and they look so ghastly, and are so changed that it is next to an impossibility to know them, although you were well acquainted with them before. I would have liked to have gone into the mad house while they were there, but the chieftain would not permit it, because they were so wild that they would have done me or any other white man an injury who ventured among them. They do the same thing to girls as well as boys.

The Eastern Siouans were inveterate gamblers. It appears, from what archaeologists and early travelers among them have noted, that the most popular game was played with fifty-one very slender reeds, each about seven inches in length. A player could throw any number of the reeds at an opponent, the purpose being to tell at a glance how many had been thrown. The game was played very swiftly until all the reeds had been discarded. Some gamblers were so skillful that they could tell accurately in an instant how many reeds an opponent had thrown. A well-made, smooth and well-polished set of reeds was highly valued and could be traded for several finely dressed doeskins. Contests resembling the game of craps also were played with dice made of animal teeth, fruit pits and stones.

8

Some characteristics of the mound-building culture were preserved in the burial practices of the Eastern Sioux long after the beginning of colonization in the Carolinas, although several centuries had elapsed since their ancestors had migrated from the valleys of middle America.

When a man died—lesser attention was paid to women unless they had distinguished themselves in some extraordinary manner—a pyramid of earth was raised, being perhaps six or eight feet in length and four feet in width. Its size depended upon the prominence of the deceased. On the top of the mound a roof, supported by poles, was constructed. From the roof eaves were hung gourds, feathers and other decorations.

The corpse was placed on a piece of bark so that the sunlight might strike it and was covered with a vermillion powder. After it had lain a day or two in the sun the carcass was removed and put upon crotched poles, and was again anointed with the powder and with oil rendered from bear's fat. This done, it was carefully wrapped in pine or cypress bark to prevent rain from falling upon it. The nearest of kin then brought the important possessions of the deceased, such as bows and arrows, beads, ornaments and his best clothing, and placed them about the body. This person, designated as the chief mourner, wore a garment of moss, and his (or her) face was blackened with pine soot and bear's oil. He dutifully recited the names of all relations of the dead man, and recounted the feats he performed in his lifetime. The chief mourner might remain beside the grave for two or three days.

From all that can be learned, it seems that a Siouan who was killed in warfare, or perished in a hunting accident, was something of a hero and was a noble and patriotic member of his tribe. Orators, usually medicine men, could be hired to sing the dead man's praises, telling, as Lawson states, "how many Enemies and Captives he had killed and taken; how strong, tall, and nimble he was; that he was a great Hunter; a Lover of his Country, and possessed of a great many beautiful Wives and Children. . . . Thus the Orator runs on, highly extolling the Dead Man for his Valor, Conduct, Strength, Riches, and Good-Humour. . . . After which he addresses himself to the People of that Town or Nation, and bids them supply the dead Man's place by following his steps . . ."

As soon as the flesh of the corpse was decomposed, it was removed from the bones and burned. The bones and the skull were thoroughly cleaned and anointed. These remains were placed in a wooden box, and once a year were rubbed with oil. Thus they were preserved for generations. It was not unusual for a person proudly and reverently to display the bones and skull of a grandfather or the skeletal remains of an ancestor of greater antiquity.

⑨ Before the beginning of the historic period in the country of the Eastern Sioux the causes of violence were more numerous than they were after the advent of colonization by European powers. Few of the prehistoric military engagements, however, can be identified as integral parts of true wars. Seldom were they encounters between territorial tribes with political unity. Moreover, conflicts involving whole tribes probably were extremely rare, simply because political and military organizations were precluded from being completely dominant by internal disruptions. Raiding parties, perhaps consisting of no more than ten to twenty warriors, or even a smaller number, were far more common than large forces.

After the arrival of white settlers, Siouan villages, bands and other entities soon came to understand that intratribal divisiveness was contributory to the economic injuries they were suffering, and that by coordination and suppression of private opinions and emotions they could defend themselves more effectively against the invaders from across the sea. Yet, their attempts to achieve this cohesiveness often were far from being successful.

Habits, customs and traditions were deeply ingrained in the Sioux. Serious troubles always had stemmed from many sources besides the desire to plunder and the determination to retaliate for an attack by external enemies, such as the Muskhogean tribes to the south and west and the Iroquois who swept down upon them from the north. Indeed, the motives for violence were so numerous and so complex that the Siouans could know no peace among themselves. Feuds were common and constant between families, clans, sibs and other types of social groups. Political rivalry and jealousy, especially among civil and military leaders, created unrest and not infrequently caused bloody clashes.

Speaking of the motives for violence, which he states "were always multiple and mixed," Driver writes:

The individual wished to enhance his personal prestige in the social hierarchy, and the band, village, or tribe wished to maintain its unity and independence as well as to improve its economic position. In addition to these general motives, desire for revenge was always present, and mere adventure should not be ruled out entirely. Although plunder in the form of weapons, food, clothing, furs, and other movables were generally taken in raids, this was not a major cause of hostilities . . . where villages were the rule, more movable goods seem to have been destroyed by fire and other means than were carried away by the victors.

Raids were never launched on the spur of the moment. Men intending to participate in a foray joined together in dancing and other ceremonies, sometimes fasted for a day or two, ingested concoctions that gave them delusions, and sought approbation and encouragement from the gods in lonely vigils. Their hair was carefully combed and freshly dressed with bear grease and red powder by women. Their entire bodies were daubed in various colors, dark red usually being applied to the face, and white and black circles being painted around the eyes. According to Lawson, for a war dance "they have a war-like Song, wherein they express, with all the Passion and Vehemence imaginable, what they intend to do with their Enemies; how they will kill, roast, scalp, beat, and make Captive, such and such Numbers of them; and how many they destroyed before."

Their vows were not merely hopes or idle threats. Captives were subjected to prolonged torture by fire, mutilation, stabbing, shooting with arrows and dismemberment while still alive. They were invariably scalped, the top of the skull sometimes being taken with the hair. Driver states that the scalps "were often given to mourners, especially to women, to dry their tears, both literally with the hair and psychologically with the feeling that revenge had been achieved." The teeth of a slain enemy were strung together to form a necklace, and his bones were valued as souvenirs.

The Eastern Sioux were savages in the basic definition of the word. It appears doubtful that they were addicted to cannibalism, like the Iroquois, who habitually roasted and feasted on the bodies of their captives, yet it is not improbable that they ate some human flesh in the wild frenzy of their victory celebrations. Many Indians believed that by drinking the blood or eating the heart of an enemy who had died bravely they would acquire some of the courage he had shown. And certainly, the Siouans preserved anatomical segments of their tortured victims as ornaments, mementos and prizes of war. Skulls and bones were publicly exhibited or proudly displayed in the houses of successful warriors.

Women and children were carried off as prisoners by raiders, but they were not mutilated. The older women were held as slaves, but attractive young women usually became wives. The children generally were adopted into the tribe of their captors. Thus the bloods of traditional enemies became mixed.

Historical records make it abundantly clear that in the first years of the colonial period most of the Siouan tribes, especially those occupying areas in the eastern parts of Virginia and the Carolinas, sought to live in peace with the European settlers. They were eager to acquire the marvels of the white man—ironware, guns, knives, clothing, blankets, horses, tools, traps and baubles that were useless but pleased the eye—and they hunted diligently to supply the furs and hides white traders demanded in exchange for these products.

The traders introduced them to rum, and soon had succeeded in making it a staple of the lucrative commerce. Lawson expressed the opinion that "most of the Savages were much addicted to Drunkenness, a Vice they never were acquainted with, till the Christians came among them. . . . In these drunken Frolicks they sometimes murder one another, fall into the fire, fall down Precipices, and break their Necks, with several other Misfortunes . . . " Among these were the biting off of noses and ears, the gouging out of eyes, and the brutal beating of women and children. If a sober Indian appeared at a trading post with furs to trade for articles he desired and refused to accept rum in exchange for them, the trader generously gave him several drinks without charge. Stimulated by the fiery liquid, his resistance broken, he willingly accepted more liquor in payment for his goods, and acquired nothing for his labors but physical torment.

Rum not only disrupted trade with the Siouans and other Indians by destroying initiative, but it was responsible for uprisings and armed clashes that seriously threatened all peaceful relationships. Bands of warriors under its influence raided settlements and Indian villages, pillaging, burning buildings and not infrequently murdering farmers and travelers.

Late in the seventeenth century, Sioux chieftains, realizing the danger to the general welfare of their people that was created by the curse, called upon the Governor of Carolina to halt the evil traffic. In response to their appeal, the colonial council passed a law forbidding the sale or giving of any strong drink to Indians, and providing a severe penalty for violations. It was wasted effort, for there was no means of enforcing the statute, and the traders continued to dispense liquor openly and without interference by authorities.

But rum, despite all the tragic episodes it brought, was not the cause of the full-scale wars that took place in the country of the Eastern Sioux in early colonial times. The main causes of these terrible conflicts, which were disastrous to the Indians, were the greed and injustice of the colonists.

The demands of traders for furs and skins created a general economic rivalry. And, as Driver notes, the acquisition of guns by Indians "made hunting so easy that large numbers of animals were killed just for their hides, the meat being left to rot or to be devoured by carnivores. Game eventually became scarce and dependence on corn increased." The Indians were cheated, charged exorbitant prices and openly robbed. Many of them became so poor and without the means of sustaining themselves as they were accustomed to do that, as Lawson states, "they had nothing more than a little moss to cover their Nakedness."

As settlement expanded, Indian lands were confiscated and the occupants driven off to wander in the wilderness or to attempt to reestablish themselves temporarily in a new location. These forced migrations created innumerable conflicts. Invariably a tribe occupying an area defended its claims, and viciously sought to drive out all intruders. It is not improbable that as many Indians were killed in fighting Indians over territorial and hunting rights as met death in warfare with whites.

Recorded history unquestionably demonstrates that for the most part the Eastern Sioux stood courageously before the onslaughts of colonial mobs and government troops. In reality, from the time of the founding of the first coastal communities, their fight had been hopeless but, of course, they could not have understood that, and even long after the fact had become apparent many of them continued to wage a brave struggle to save at least parts of their homelands. For many years, man for man, bow for bow, gun for gun, they were a match for their antagonists. They achieved victories, but only on the field of battle, for they had no recourse in statutes, not even an opportunity to assert their rights before a so-called court of justice. For them there was neither a judicial tribunal willing to consider their pleas nor justice.

In the end they were overwhelmed by forces numerically greater than they could muster and by the appearance of superior weapons in the form of breech-loading guns and firepower in metal cartridges. Tribe after tribe retreated and vanished, until at last those who had not been slain or enslaved had become scattered and completely disorganized, driven beyond the point of no return—to oblivion.

10   Nothing is known of the MONETON as an individual tribe after the year 1674, when a trader, Gabriel Arthur, visited them in what he called "a great town," believed to have been located on the Kanawha River or one of its tributaries. They may have been driven from this location by the Iroquois, or possibly by the Conoy or some other Algonquian people. In any case, they scattered, and it is believed they were absorbed by various Siouan tribes of the Virginian Piedmont.

The size of their population is unknown, and no song, story or place name commemorates them.

11 The MANAHOAC dominated a loose confederacy in Virginia. Besides the Manahoac proper, the subdivisions were the Hassinunga, Ontponea, Shackaconia, Stegaraki, Tanxnitania, Tegninateo and Whonkentia. They were also allies of the Monacan.

The first white man known to have encountered them was the famed explorer John Smith. He found them in 1608 in various areas of the Potomac River watershed. They were at the time at war with the Algonquian Powhatan and the Iroquoian Susquehanna. The latter tribe undoubtedly drove them southward about the middle of the seventeenth century. Some of them, perhaps a majority, settled on the upper James River. They were strong enough to defeat a large force comprised of both white soldiers and Indian mercenaries which was sent by the colonial government of Virginia to drive them from this area. In time, however, the confederacy was broken. The Stegaraki and the Ontponea lived for a few years in the vicinity of Fort Christanna, in the present Brunswick County. Ethnologists believe that all remnants of the Manahoac Confederacy eventually were united with the Tutelo and Saponi, and thus the name disappeared from history.

Authorities estimate that the population of the Manahoac was 1,500 at the beginning of the seventeenth century. Fifty years later only between 600 and 700 survived, but these figures may have included some Tutelo and Saponi. The Manahoac are not remembered by a place name.

12   Only one small town in Goochland County, Virginia, perpetuates the name of the MONACAN, and it is misspelled as *Manakin*. Investigating the country of the upper James River in 1807, the doughty Capt. John Smith came upon several of their villages, and marked "the country of the Monacans" on a map. Most of them were driven from the area in the next few years. Colonists confiscated their valuable agricultural lands. A few of them were reported to be camping in adjacent territory as late as the first two years of the eighteenth century, but they were a destroyed people. The ultimate fate of the remnants was not recorded, but it is believed that they took refuge among the Saponi and Tutelo when these tribes sought protection at Fort Christanna. Probably no more than one hundred Monacan were living in 1700.

13 Disease and warfare with white men took a heavy toll of the NAHYSSAN. They were driven from their homes in the area of Petersburg, Virginia, by the Iroquoian Susquehanna. About 1654 they were at the falls of James River, and although greatly depleted in number they demonstrated their prowess as warriors by defeating troops and settlers sent against them by the colonial government. They moved to the junction of the Dan and Staunton rivers about 1675, but a few years later the survivors had united with other Siouan groups on the upper Yadkin River in North Carolina, and their name as a tribe was lost to history.

14   A traveler, John Lederer, made several journeys in the vicinity of the border between North Carolina and Virginia late in the seventeenth century. He met the OCCANEECHI on the Roanoke River in the present Mecklenburg County, and described them as being very influential in both economic and religious affairs. They were, Lederer asserted, noted throughout the region as traders, and the Siouan dialect they spoke was the common speech both of trade and religion over a considerable area. If correct, this would indicate that in attaining such prominence they had lived there a considerable number of years. Reports that their main town was on an island in the Roanoke River had circulated as early as 1650, but they probably occupied the site, or an adjacent location, long before that time. Some Saponi and Tutelo dwelt on nearby islands.

About 1676 a band of Conestoga [a branch of the Iroquoian Susquehanna], perhaps separated from their own people by political or religious difference, asked for sanctuary among the Occaneechi and their request was granted. Undoubtedly the Occaneechi were glad to increase their manpower. They made a mistake in being hospitable, however, for the Conestoga, like all people of Iroquoian blood, proved to be treacherous and disloyal to their benefactors, and the Occaneechi were obliged to drive them out of the area.

Attacks by both colonists and other Iroquois forced the Occaneechi to flee southward. According to Lawson, they were living on the Eno River in Orange County, North Carolina, in 1701. William Byrd, in a regional history, asserts that they united with the Saponi, whose name they adopted.

But the name Occaneechi did not disappear entirely from history immediately after this amalgamation. Undoubtedly because of the far-ranging trading missions they conducted, a main trade route that extended from Petersburg, Virginia, southwestward into South Carolina continued to be known for many years as the Occaneechi Trail.

15 If the accounts of early colonists are only partially accurate, the SAPONI were one of the most itinerant of the Eastern Siouan tribes. Their wanderings, however, were not undertaken by choice. They suffered adversities that swiftly destroyed people of less stamina and courage. Indeed, diseases and warfare with both other Indians and colonists took such a heavy toll it seems miraculous that a handful of them were still among the living at the middle of the eighteenth century.

Their places of residence—all of which were temporary—might be likened to the schedule of a hypothetical railroad running between South Carolina and Canada. The following itinerary probably does not include all the locations in which they sought survival:

The Rivanna River in Albemarle County, Virginia. Located here by Captain John Smith early in the seventeenth century.

Otter Creek southwest of Lynchburg, Virginia, a few years later.

An island in the Roanoke River in Mecklenburg County, Virginia, about 1675.

A few years later, on the Yadkin River near Salisbury, North Carolina. Lawson found them here in 1701.

Wandering through Virginia in the first decade of the eighteenth century.

By 1711 back in North Carolina, west of Windsor in Bertie County.

Next, a few years later in Brunswick County, Virginia.

Then, shortly afterward, some of them were in Nottoway County, Virginia.

By 1740—several years after the Iroquois had ceased to attack Virginia Indians—both Saponi and the Tutelo were living together near Shamokin, Pennsylvania. Not all of the Saponi chose to go so far north. One band stopped in Granville County, North Carolina.

In 1753 the Iroquoian Cayuga adopted both the Saponi

and the Tutelo; but they remained apart from the Cayuga, their main village being at the time near Ithaca, New York.

In 1778 a Saponi group lived on the upper waters of the Susquehanna River, in New York.

The Saponi separated from the Tutelo at Niagara in 1779.

In 1780 some Saponi lived with the Cayuga on the Seneca River, in New York.

Other Saponi who had dwelt in various places in North Carolina became united with the Tuscarora, Meherrin and Machapunga and moved north with these people in 1802.

Actually, their identity as a tribe had ended long before this time. In 1765 there were only thirty Saponi warriors known to be living on the Susquehanna River in New York. One small band still living in North Carolina in 1755 was comprised of fourteen men and fourteen women, and an unknown number of children. Another North Carolina band contained twenty warriors, and an indeterminable number of women and children.

It is doubtful if any full-blood Saponi were alive after the beginning of the nineteenth century.

In Davidson County, North Carolina, a village called Sapona remains the only memorial to a once strong and brave people.

16 On February 17, 1935, an aged TUTELO whose Siouan name was *Ga-poga-tadyi* died on the Canadian Iroquois Reserve, in Brant County, Ontario. Only five days earlier he had completed a series of disc recordings of aboriginal Tutelo liturgies for the ethnologists F. G. and F. S. Speck, of the University of Pennsylvania. In this priceless collection are preserved the religious songs and ceremonial chants of the Eastern Siouans.

"I may add," F. G. Speck wrote in 1935, "that the Tutelo descendants in Ontario still remember definitely something of their Carolinian and Virginian traditions and still consider themselves southerners by origin." And the eminent Indian scholar of the Bureau of American Ethnology, John R. Swanton, states that the Tutelo "are noteworthy chiefly as the principal body of Siouan Indians from Virginia to retain their integrity and to preserve a knowledge of their language late enough for a permanent record of it to be made."

There is no English equivalent, as F. G. Speck notes, for the name *Ga-poga-tadyi*, "because the title is a Tutelo term whose meaning has been forgotten." *Ga-poga-tadyi*, a descendant of a long line of Tutelo chieftains, was popularly known as John Buck. But if the meaning of his name had been forgotten, he had not forgotten the traditions and the documented history of his people, and he took great pride in relating them as his personal contribution to science.*

From their earliest known Virginia home on the Big Sandy River, the Tutelo moved to an island in the Roanoke River, adjacent to the island home of the Occaneechi. It is ironical that they were driven from this location by the Iroquois, among whom the tribe would spend the last two and a half centuries of its existence. They drifted toward the

---

*No more than seven Tutelo families were still alive in the late 1930s, and very few members, if any, of this group, were purebloods.

southwest, and Lawson located them on the upper Yadkin River in 1701.

Although both the Tutelo and the Saponi (the latter by this time a very small group) had been granted membership as "younger brothers" in the League of the Iroquois, they chose to live apart from their adopters and lived with or close to each other in Tioga County, Pennsylvania, and Tompkins County, New York. The Revolutionary War brought drastic changes. The American general, John Sullivan, destroyed the Tutelo and Saponi towns. The alliance was forever broken, and the Tutelo joined the Cayuga who fled to Canada. In Ontario they still continued to live apart from the Cayuga, retaining their identity as a separate tribe and speaking their own language almost until the beginning of the twentieth century. Thereafter they became, in effect, a branch of the Canadian Iroquois, the bloods of the two people fused, although, as previously cited, liturgies of Tutelo origin are still a part of Iroquoian religious ceremonials. The Tutelo as a people, however, have long been gone.

17   For a few years early in the eighteenth century the KEY-
AUWEE, facing annihilation by the Iroquois, took refuge
among several other Siouan groups, among them parts of
the Tutelo, Saponi, Occaneechi and Shakori, in the vicinity
of Albemarle Sound, North Carolina. In 1716, Governor
Alexander Spotswood of Virginia proposed that the Keyauwee, Eno and Cheraw tribes be settled on a permanent
reservation on the frontier of North Carolina. The North
Carolina government opposed the plan, and it was not
carried out.

    Homeless and unwanted, the Keyauwee and the Cheraw
joined forces and moved southward. They lived on the Pee
Dee River, on the border between North and South Carolina
as late as 1761, but soon after this year they became
scattered and disappeared from history. It is possible some
of them were absorbed by the Catawba. Swanton notes that
some of their descendants were found among Indians of
Robeson County, North Carolina, who were mistakenly
called Croatan. No tribe with this name existed.

18   On his sight-seeing journey of 1701, John Lawson recorded a few words of the WOCCON dialect when he was among them, presumably in Wayne County, North Carolina. Why he chose to write this brief vocabulary, and to ignore the dialects of other Siouan tribes he encountered is not known, but his efforts greatly aided linguists, for the words showed that the Woccon language was close to that of the Catawba, one of the largest Siouan tribes, a vocabulary of which also exists. Lawson's little dictionary—it contained only 113 words—revealing as it was, posed some problems that have not been resolved, and created controversies among scientists. Catawba groups were scattered throughout North and South Carolina, and some resided in Tennessee. Who were the latter people who had chosen to remain in their ancient homes in midland America instead of migrating eastward with their relatives? At least one prominent anthropologist, Douglas L. Rights, suggests that the Woccon were originally Waccamaw, and there is circumstantial geographical evidence, if little else, to support his theory. (See Waccamaw.)

No Woccon survived long enough to solve the mysteries. In 1711, the Iroquoian Tuscarora who had suffered from kidnappings, enslavement and confiscation of their lands by white settlers, induced the Woccon and several tribes to join them in launching a strong offensive against their persecutors.

In fierce fighting more than two hundred colonists were slain before troops from North and South Carolina and Virginia succeeded in halting the uprising.

The warfare doomed the Woccon as a tribe. Most of them were killed, and the few survivors scattered among the Catawba and some other peoples, never to be heard of again.

19 Two traders, James Needham and Gabriel Arthur, discovered the YADKIN on the upper waters of a river to which they gave the same name in western North Carolina sometime in 1674. Nearly thirty years passed before they were again mentioned in history by the peripatetic Lawson under the name of Reatkin.

Then followed an even longer period of silence. And it still continues. They vanished from the Yadkin River Valley, and nothing is known of their fate.

But, strangely, their name is preserved with greater prominence than many much larger Siouan tribes. A prehistoric culture of the Piedmont was named for them, and they are commemorated in North Carolina by Yadkin River, Yadkin County, Yadkin College, Yadkin Falls, Yadkin Valley and Yadkinville.

20 If the CAPE FEAR INDIANS possessed a Siouan name, it has never come to light. Indeed, they might not have been a tribe in their own right. There is reason to believe that they may have been a branch of the Waccamaw, with whom they are known to have been closely associated. They were named by early voyagers, who first encountered them in the Cape Fear vicinity.

In 1661 a company of settlers from New England attempted to establish a colony on the Cape Fear River. According to Swanton, they seized a number of Indian children "and sent them away under pretense of instructing them in the ways of civilization." This was a serious mistake, for a number of the colonists were killed, and the remainder narrowly escaped the same fate only by sailing away. Two other attempts to plant settlements in the area, in 1663 and 1665, also met with failure.

Governor Archdale of North Carolina succeeded in making peace with the Cape Fear Indians a short time later, pledging himself to protect them from both Indian and white enemies. For several years they remained loyal allies of the colonial government, served as scouts for North Carolina forces in the Tuscarora uprising and protected the Point Royal region.

Then, as was the case of all other Indians who trusted the whites, the colonists turned on them, confiscated their lands and drove them out. The Iroquois barred their way to the north, and between 1716 and 1720, they sought to escape complete disaster by moving south. They found a haven in Williamsburg County, South Carolina. Little is known of them during the next several decades, but between 1780 and 1790 some were living with a small Pedee band and a few others were with the Catawba.

It is not believed that any Cape Fear Indian survived the end of the eighteenth century.

21   The chronology of the CATAWBA, probably the largest of the Eastern Siouan tribes, is a tale of tragedies. They were, with a short-lived exception, faithful friends of the colonists, and they paid dearly for this loyalty.

They served with white forces in 1711–1713 against the Iroquoian Tuscarora, at whose hands they had suffered for years. Some of them participated in the Yamasee uprising, but their hearts were not in the fight, and they soon returned to peaceful ways.

But there was no peace for them. Their only reward for assisting the whites came in the form of liquor, venereal diseases and other afflictions. They were almost constantly attacked, if not by the Iroquois, then by the Shawnee and the Delaware.

In 1738 smallpox took the lives of a large number of them. In 1759 the same diseases again swept through their villages, killing half of them.

In the hope of escaping the virulent ravages, they moved southward from their old homes in North Carolina to South Carolina, but the migration benefited them not at all. The South Carolina colonial government assigned a tract of land fifteen miles square to them in 1762, but by this time their spirit was broken, they were desultory farmers, and easy prey for unscrupulous traders who flooded their reservation with liquor.

They sank into relative insignificance, seemingly unable to revive the pride they had once possessed or to maintain their traditional faith. Although their sympathies were with the colonists in the Revolutionary War, they had no heart for fighting, and they fled into the wilderness of western Virginia to avoid clashing with the British, returning to their reservation after the battle of Guilford Court House.

The South Carolina government, soon thereafter, confiscated nearly all Catawba lands—which had been awarded to them in perpetuity—calling the action "leasing." Seeking to rid itself of them forever, South Carolina now forced them to "sell" all the reservation, and falsely promised to obtain other lands for them in their former home of North Carolina. North Carolina, of course, did not want them back, and the promise could not be fulfilled. Thus stymied, South Carolina generously set aside eight hundred acres for them. Although this was called their "home," they were, for all intents and purposes, homeless. Most of them—undoubtedly more than the land would support—remained on the eight hundred acres. Indeed, some of them are still crowded upon it, but South Carolina consistently has refused to increase the size of the plot. Compassion and generosity are not characteristics of this backward state. Indians are still not wanted, even if it is reluctantly admitted—but only under the force of federal statutes—that they and blacks are human beings. When it comes to appropriations for anthropology, archaeology, ethnology, sanitation and social problems, South Carolina is noted for its niggardliness.

It is improbable that any Eastern Siouan tribes became as widely scattered as the Catawba. Some went to live with the Cherokee. Some went as far west as Oklahoma and found homes among the Choctaw. Some went to Arkansas and to Colorado. A few families went to Utah and became converted into the Mormon faith. All of these wanderers had with them individuals and perhaps families from smaller Siouan tribes which also had been driven out of their homelands.

Besides place names in at least ten states, including South Carolina, the Catawba have one other claim to fame. A variety of grape was named for them.

22 Columbia, the capital of South Carolina, was at one time called CONGAREE, after the Siouan tribe that ranged through the South Carolina Piedmont. Lawson, who encountered them in 1701 on the Santee River, spoke of them as "having lost much of their former Numbers, by intestine Broils, but most of them by the Small-pox, which hath often visited them. The Congarees are kind and affable to the English . . ." He mentioned the "abundance of Storks and Cranes in their Savannas. They take them before they cane fly, and breed them as tame and familiar as a Dung-hill-Fowl. They had a tame Crane at one of these Cabins, that was scarcely less than six foot in Height, his Head being round, with a shining, natural Crimson Hue. . . . These are a very Comely Sort of Indians. . . . The Women here being as handsome as most I have met withal, being several fine fingered Brounettos amongst them."

The settlers repaid the friendliness of the Congaree with brutal treatment by stealing their resources. In desperate condition, they at last took to the warpath, in 1715 participating in the abortive Yamasee uprising. Many were slain in the fighting. Colonists confiscated their lands, and sent almost all of them to the West Indies as slaves.

Those who escaped fled to the Catawba. In 1715 it was estimated that only about forty Congaree men, women and children were alive. Soon thereafter their name as a tribe had vanished, but the colonists who stole their lands did perpetuate it by naming the Congaree River after them.

23   The PEDEE, once a strong and capable tribe, were so deci-
mated by the diseases of Europeans that white traders
generally avoided the country they occupied in their miserable state along the Great Pee Dee River. Probably as the
result of excessive imbibing, a few of them in 1744 joined a
small group of Natchez in attacking and killing several
Catawba. In retaliation the Catawba drove them from their
homes. The Pedee sued for peace. It was granted, and most
of the Pedee were absorbed by the Catawba. Some of them,
however, went to live in white settlements, earning a bare
living as menials or, more properly speaking, as slaves.

No full-blood Pedee is known to have survived the end of
the eighteenth century.

24 The SANTEE, who dwelt on the river bearing their name, sent warriors to aid the colonists in their campaign against the Iroquoian Tuscarora in 1711. This was a defensive action taken in their own behalf, but four years later they turned on the whites, undoubtedly for a similar reason. In 1716 they were attacked and defeated by a combined force of colonial troops and Muskhogean Indians. Most of them were sold into slavery in the West Indies. The few survivors—perhaps eighty men, women and children—vanished.

25 A fantastic tale has come down through early accounts about the SEWEE. They dwelt along the coast, on the lower Santee River and on Seewee Bay (now called Bulls Bay), and they were probably the first Indians encountered by the British who founded the colony of South Carolina. They were friendly with the colonists, and a considerable trade developed.

Steadily the number of ships arriving and departing for England increased through the years. At last some enterprising Sewee, whose name, unfortunately, is unknown, conceived a plan with which he believed the British traders could be outwitted. They were, he charged, cheating the Sewee, and the only way his people could obtain a fair share of the lucrative commerce was to transport the furs, skins and other products the traders wanted directly across the water and exchange them for pots, clothing and guns in European ports.

The operation was readily approved by the Sewee council. Enthusiasm ran high, for it believed that profits could be increased twenty fold by eliminating the colonial middleman. All that was needed to assure success was to build much larger canoes than those used on the bays and rivers along the coast . . . or so it was thought.

The work was carried on in secret. Just how many of the "seagoing" canoes were constructed is not a matter of record, but there must have been quite a few of them, and the complement of each must have been large, for the tribe was virtually wiped out by the experiment. One account states that only minors, cripples and the elderly were left at home.

The fleet, propelled by square mat sails, had been embarked on the voyage only two days when a storm struck. A British vessel that happened to come along at the time rescued about half of the Sewee sailors and carried them off to the West Indies, where they were sold as slaves. All others perished at sea.

According to Swanton, only fifty-seven Sewee were known to be alive in 1715.

26 The WAXHAW may have been closely related to the Catawba. According to Lawson, they were called *Flatheads* by other tribes, "which seems a very suitable Name for them. In their Infancy, their Nurses lay the Back-part of their Children's Heads on a Bag of Sand . . ." Very soon after it is born, "an infant is laid with its Back on a flat Board, and swaddled hard down thereon, from one end of this Engine to the other. This method makes the Child's Body and limbs as straight as an Arrow."

Apparently after the Yamasee uprising, the Waxhaw were living with, or close to, the Catawba (q.v.). Angered at their refusal to make peace with the English, the Catawba killed almost all of them in a bloody "family row." A few survivors fled to the Cheraw, while one small band went to Florida, where they were last heard of in 1720.

27 The WACCAMAW tribe was scattered and broken early in colonial times. Some of them joined the Cheraw in attacking white settlements in 1715, but the fighting was of short duration. Five years later Waccamaw again went on the warpath against colonists, but were badly beaten, some of them being captured and sold as slaves. As previously stated, the so-called Cape Fear Indians (q.v.) may have been a branch of the Waccamaw. In 1755 a band of Cherokee and Natchez killed a number of Waccamaw. The ultimate fate of the Waccamaw is in doubt. It seems obvious that the few who still survived in the middle of the eighteenth century became mixed with other tribes.

28 The CHERAW were deadly enemies of the English, and consistently rejected all overtures of peace. Their greatest claim to distinction, however, is found in the fact that they are the only Eastern Siouan tribe definitely identifiable in the accounts of the De Soto expedition. The Spanish conquistador spent four days among them in 1540.

The noted authority, Swanton, states that about 1700 they moved northward near the southern border of Virginia. There they came under constant attack by the Iroquois, and a decade later they moved southeast and united with the Keyauwee. According to Swanton, North Carolina declared war on the Cheraw, "and applied to Virginia for assistance. This Governor Spotswood refused, as he believed the Carolinians were the aggressors, but the contest was prosecuted by the latter. . . . During this period complaint was made that the Cheraw were responsible for most of the depredations committed north of Santee River and they were accused of trying to draw the coast tribes into an alliance with them. It was asserted also that arms were being supplied them from Virginia."

Between 1726 and 1729 the Cheraw united with the Catawba. The last historical notice of them appeared in 1768, at which time the few still alive were among the Catawba.

29   The ENO valiantly fought early Spanish expeditions. In the early years of the British colonies they moved northward from South Carolina along the foot of the Appalachian Mountains after forming an alliance with the Shakori, Tutelo, Saponi, Occaneechi and the Keyauwee. North Carolina did not want them, claiming that the Eno, Cheraw and Keyauwee were at war with South Carolina. The alliance disintegrated but the Eno and Shakori stayed together. At one time they lived in a town called Adshusheer, near the present Hillsboro, North Carolina. Owing to the unfriendliness of the North Carolina colonial government, they returned to South Carolina and lived a precarious existence. They may have joined the Catawba, but by the middle of the eighteenth century they had disappeared from history.

30 The SHAKORI will always have a place in history, for they gave their name to the legendary province of Chicora, whence came the Indian slave Chicora, who excited and charmed the Spanish Court early in the sixteenth century with fabulous tales of his homeland.

It is probable they abandoned their South Carolina territory and moved far inland to escape Spanish expeditions.

They were long united with the Eno (q.v.).

31 The SISSIPAHAW were mentioned under the name of *Sauxpa* in the records of the expedition of 1569, led by the Spanish conquistador, Juan Pardo. For a century and a half thereafter only vague references about them appear. It is believed they were closely related to the Shakori, and at one time the two tribes may have been united.

The Sissipahaw took part in the Yamasee uprising against the English in 1715, but nothing more of their fate is known. It is possible they were absorbed by the Catawba.

32   The SUGAREE first came upon the stage of history in 1701, when Lawson mentioned them. The role they played was minor, and they disappeared as abruptly as they had appeared. Colonial warfare and intertribal fighting probably took a heavy toll of them, and the few who escaped death may have taken refuge among some band of the Catawba. Nothing more definite is known of them.

33 In 1567 the WATEREE wiped out the garrison of a small Spanish fort on the Cherokee frontier in far northwestern South Carolina. A hundred years later Lawson met them on the river bearing their name. He didn't think much of them, writing that they were "great Pilferers, stealing from us any Thing they could lay their Hands on, though very respectful in giving us what Victuals we wanted. We lay in their Cabins all night, being dark smoky Holes as ever I saw any Indians dwell in." Some of them joined the colonial forces in fighting the Tuscarora in 1711. Swanton states that the "Yamasee War reduced their power considerably." In 1744 they sold the lands they claimed between the Congaree and Wateree rivers to a white trader. Then they, too, disappeared into bands of the Catawba Tribe.

34   Strangely, the WINYAW are not mentioned in colonial records until 1670, although there seems to be little doubt that long before the discovery of America they were living on the coast of the state that would one day be called South Carolina.

They were still in this location in 1683, when colonists raided them for slaves on the false pretext that they had killed a white man.

They were still in South Carolina—at least the small number still alive were—in 1715, for in that year the Cheraw failed in an attempt to induce them to fight against the colonists in the Yamasee war.

Some reports state that they fought with white settlers against their relatives, the Waccamaw, but this seems doubtful. Certainly they did not participate in this fighting as a tribe, because about this time they united with the Waccamaw. And that is the last heard of them.

35 There is no means of tabulating the populations of the individual Eastern Siouan tribes at the beginning of the historical period, or, actually, at any time in the following two hundred years. An uncountable number of mergers took place in this period. Some tribes were virtually annihilated in warfare between whites and Indians and between Indians and Indians. Others were largely wiped out by European diseases. Many were carried away as slaves.

The earliest population figures which may be considered in any degree reliable indicate that by about 1600 the population of all Eastern Siouan tribes in Virginia, North Carolina and South Carolina was slightly less than 25,000 men, women and children.*

EASTERN SIOUAN PLACE NAMES

TRIBE	PLACE NAME
Monacan	Village called Manakin, in Virginia.
Saponi	Village called Sapona, in North Carolina.
Cape Fear Indians	Cape Fear and Cape Fear River, in North Carolina.
Cheraw	Suwali Gap in the Blue Ridge Mountains, Saura Town Mountains, Uwaharrie River, Uwaharrie Mountains, all in North Carolina. The town of Cheraw in South Carolina.
Eno	Eno River and the village of Enno in

*Needless to say, it is not possible to determine with any degree of accuracy whatsoever the population of any prehistoric people. The earliest information available is found in statements—most of them no more than guesses —of explorers, missionaries, traders and military and civil officials. For population figures in this work I have relied mainly on two authorities who made studies on the subject, Drs. James Mooney and John R. Swanton of the Bureau of American Ethnology.

	North Carolina. Enoree River in South Carolina.
Shakori	Shocco and Big Shocco Creeks in North Carolina.
Sissipahaw	The towns of Saxapaha and Haw River, in North Carolina.
Yadkin	Yadkin College, and the towns of Yadkin Falls, Yadkin Valley, and Yadkinville, and Yadkin River, all in North Carolina.
Catawba	Catawba River and Catawba Reservoir in North and South Carolina, and the towns of Catawba in North Carolina, Virginia, West Virginia, Kentucky, Ohio, Missouri, New York, Oklahoma, South Carolina and Wisconsin, and an island in the Ohio River.
Congaree	Congaree River and village of same name in South Carolina.
Pedee	The village of Pee Dee, and the Great and Little Pee Dee rivers in South Carolina.
Santee	The village of Santee and the Santee River in South Carolina.
Waccamaw	Waccamaw River in North and South Carolina, and a lake of the same name in North Carolina.
Wateree	Wateree River and the town of Wateree in South Carolina.
Waxhaw	The village of Waxhaw, and Waxhaw Creek in South Carolina.
Winyaw	Winyaw Bay in South Carolina.

The names of the Moneton, Manahoac, Nahyssan, Occaneechi, Tutelo, Keyauwee, Woccon, Sewee and Sugaree have not been preserved in place names.

PART THREE

The Southern Sioux

1 In the fall of 1669, René-Robert Cavalier, Sieur de La Salle, was pushing southward from Lake Erie into country never before seen by a European. He was accompanied by a few French-Canadian watermen—perhaps no more than six or eight—and a Shawnee hunter-guide whom he called Niki. His objective was to explore a river which some Seneca Iroquois who visited his trading post during the previous winter had told him had its headwaters in their country, "attained a size beyond calculation, and flowed in the course the sun moved."

So far distant was the end of this river, said the Senecas, "that a journey of eight or nine moons would be required to reach it." They had heard that at last it disappeared into a sea that stretched to the horizon, and the waters of this sea "were warm and of a reddish color." The Senecas spoke the river's name as *Ohio*, which meant "beautiful," "fair" or "fine," however one wished to use it.

. . . a sea of warm waters of a reddish color.

La Salle was filled with intense excitement. These descriptive words warranted the assumption—which in his deliberations had soon been elevated to a conviction—that the mouth of the Ohio was upon the Gulf of California, known to him by the name *Vermillion Sea*.

Ever since the voyages of Columbus, adventurers striking (along the immense land mass of North America) had been dominated by a dream of finding a water passage through it. Each search had ended against impregnable coasts. Now the old dream had been given new life in La Salle by indubitable geographical and historical factors. First, there was the water route up the St. Lawrence to the Great Lakes. From Lake Erie, the Senecas had told him, it was possible to travel up smaller streams and to descend others *within their own country*, to reach the great river. The land through which the Ohio passed had not always been *their own country*. La Salle, an insatiable student of Indians, knew that when the Senecas had been discovered by fur traders their homeland had been in western New York, between Seneca Lake and the Geneva River. Only about two decades before 1666, the year in which he himself had reached Canada at the age of twenty-two, the Iroquois had launched their bloody westward aggressions. They had in time conquered numerous tribes in New York, Pennsylvania, Ohio, Indiana, Michigan and other areas. These offensives had enabled the Seneca to become the westernmost tribe of the Iroquois nation, and they had established their villages along Lake Erie and on streams to the south of it. The region called Ohio had become Iroquois Country.

La Salle found the Beautiful River of the Senecas. Somewhere in the Valley of the Ohio all his companions, except Niki, deserted him. La Salle refused to turn back. He and the Shawnee went on downstream in a small canoe, but as the year neared an end they found themselves at the head of strong rapids. They had reached the site of Louisville. There his dream was shattered. Some Indians he encountered— perhaps a band of wandering Shawnee hunters—made it clear to him that the Ohio emptied into an even larger river, and that Indian people dwelling on its banks called it by a name that sounded like Mississippi.

La Salle was well versed in the history of the Spanish on the Mississippi. It had been marked on Spanish maps for considerably more than a hundred years. If the distance they had advanced up it remained indeterminate, they controlled its lower reaches at least, and the prospect of imprisonment and possible execution at their hands convinced him of the wisdom of turning back.*

As far as the story of the Sioux is concerned, La Salle's discovery of the Ohio River and his journey through the Ohio Country is important for the reason that he apparently did not encounter any Siouan people. In later reports he identified a number of tribes destroyed by Iroquoian wolfpacks on their rampages through the Midwest, but the list contains only one name that can be definitely associated with a Siouan people. That name is *Mosopolea,* and its inclusion is a mistake.

The Siouan tribes of the Ohio Valley were not destroyed but were driven out by the Iroquois. If any Siouan tribe was annihilated by these murdering legions, it was so insignificant that no record of it has come down through history.

The Siouans who remained in this area of middle America long after

---

*Francis Parkman believed that La Salle continued down the Ohio to its confluence with the Mississippi, but available evidence does not unequivocably substantiate such a contention.

the eastern migrations had taken place eventually were forced to flee, but there was no mass exodus. Some tribes departed together, and others moved out alone, all keeping ahead of the powerful forces from the northeast—who were armed with guns obtained from Dutch, British and French traders—and whose way of life was warfare, killing for the pleasure they found in it.

It is apparent, therefore, that all Siouans were gone from the Ohio Valley by the early 1600s. While most of them went northward from the mouth of the Ohio River, at least four tribes turned southward, to become the southern branch of the great broken family.

2 The Southern Siouan tribes, and their first definitely known historical homelands were:

BILOXI: On the Alabama River in Wilcox County, Alabama.

QUAPAW: At the junction of the Mississippi and Arkansas Rivers, in both Arkansas and Mississippi.

MOSOPELEA: On the Cumberland River in Kentucky.

PASCAGOULA: On the River named for them, in Mississippi, about twenty to thirty miles above its mouth on the Gulf of Mexico.

MOCTOBI: Probably a branch of the Biloxi.

3 The BILOXI have long been in Limbo but, as everyone knows who has traveled along the Gulf of Mexico coast, their name has survived them. But it is preserved not only in a city, a bay and countless business establishments. It lives in history, for they were the first Indians met in 1699 by Pierre Lemoyne, Sieur d'Iberville, the founder of Louisiana, and the first two capitals of the colony, Old and New Biloxi, were named for them.

Some anthropologists have expressed the belief that they had at one time lived near the Susquehanna River—at what point is uncertain—and are the same people called Capitanesses on early Dutch charts of the southern Pennsylvania and northern Maryland region. Obviously not all of the tribe were settled on the Gulf of Mexico coast when Sieur d'Iberville landed, for in 1733 there was a Biloxi village near the town of Clifton on the Alabama River. When this village was established, or how long it existed, is not known, but it is improbable that it was occupied for any great length of time. Most likely it was no more than a place in which a part of the Biloxi resided during their migration to join the others who had preceded them and had established themselves on the lower Pascagoula River. Ordinarily Indian migrations covering such a great distance progress slowly—if the Biloxi did not come from Pennsylvania or Maryland, they at least moved southward from the Ohio Valley.

It seems that, like other Siouan tribes, the Biloxi were forced to move by enemies, if not by the Iroquois, then by some other people. When they first reached the Gulf is, of course, a matter that cannot be determined by scientific evidence. The prominence accorded them in the accounts of Sieur d'Iberville, however, indicate that they were well established and influential.

As far as is known, from the time of their arrival in the Deep South the Biloxi were so closely associated with the Pascagoula that there is reason to believe they were related.

This is a subject that will be given further treatment in commenting on the history of the Pascagoula.

The origin of the name Biloxi is believed to be a corruption of their own name, Taneks anya, as Swanton states, "filtered over the tongues of other Indians." In its corrupt form, Biloxi may have originated from words that meant "first people." Hodge suggests that it was "apparently from the Choctaw language." His theory may have stemmed from a long prevailing belief that the Biloxi belonged to the southern branch of the Muskhogean linguistic family, of which the Choctaw were members. In 1886, however, the ethnologist Albert S. Gatchet visited survivors of the Biloxi in Louisiana and found that many words of their language were Siouan. His discovery was confirmed a few years later by J. Owen Dorsey of the American Bureau of Ethnology.

Although only a few Biloxi still lived in Louisiana in 1892, when Dorsey confirmed their linguistic affiliation, he was able to gain considerable information about their prehistoric culture. He concluded that before the first white men reached the region Biloxi men wore the breechcloth, a belt, leggings, moccasins and garters. It was thought that the women wore a short skirt of dressed doeskin. Both sexes covered themselves with soft skin robes in cold weather, and adorned themselves with feather capes and hairpieces, necklaces of animal and bird bones, bills of some species of a long-legged redbird (possibly the flamingo) and noserings and earrings made of various materials.

Interestingly, Hodge adds that the dwellings of the Biloxi "resembled those of the northern tribes of the same family, one kind similar to the low tent of the Osage and Winnebago, the other like the high tent of the Dakota, Omaha, and others." Thus, even though they had become Southern Indians of the Gulf Coast and tidal swamplands, they largely had retained their traditional type of housing. But this was not true of many of their customs. In the North, for example, they had made pottery, but the art was abandoned when they reached the South. There they made utensils of wood, and with the material readily obtainable they wove excellent baskets for storage and transport. One social custom that was continued to the very end was their reckoning of descent through the female line. Another was an elaborate and complicated clan system, but Dorsey was able to learn the names of only three of them, which to white tongues are virtually unpronounceable.

The Biloxi route to the South is delineated by only the single village near Clifton, Alabama, but it seems apparent that they struck more or less directly southward from the Ohio Valley, and followed a land trail. If they had been in danger of being attacked by Iroquois, there would have been no reason to have traveled rapidly after passing through Kentucky. It is probable that they had friends, or even relatives, in both Kentucky and Tennessee. No one can say, however, what perils, if any, they encountered south of the latter state.

Even more important, no one can say what prompted them to continue their journey until they had traveled the length of Alabama and turned westward to the Pascagoula River in Mississippi. There must have been a reason why they spent years filtering through the great Southern forests to reach this goal. Why didn't they go west or north to join other Siouan tribes? Any number of theories can be advanced, but they would be meaningless without material support. The explanation will be forever shrouded in mystery.

The founding of the Colony of Louisiana brought French traders into the region. Sieur d'Iberville had first encountered the Biloxi on the bay named for them, but when he returned to the area in the following year the village he had visited was deserted. It was learned in time that they had moved to live with the Pascagoula on the Pascagoula River, a journey of nearly three days—presumably by water—to the northeast. Traders sought them out and established commercial relations with them.

This trade must have been profitable, for when New Orleans was established in 1718 by Jean Baptiste Lemoyne, Sieur de Bienville, the Biloxi were persuaded to move near to it. Apparently this resulted in disagreements, for the Biloxi lived on a bayou near New Orleans less than four years. In 1722 they built a new village on Pearl River on lands formerly occupied about two decades earlier by the Muskhogean Acolapissa, who had moved west of the Mississippi. In this location, the Biloxi, and probably most of the Pascagoula, dwelt for approximately forty years.

It would appear that these people greatly depended on the French for both trade and protection. Soon after 1763, when French rule east of the Mississippi ended, they moved westward into Louisiana and occupied territory on the Red River, in the vicinity of Marksville. In the late years of the eighteenth century they moved two more times, first farther up the Red River, and then to Bayou Boeuf.

By 1800 the pressures of civilization were disrupting their way of life to the extent that they decided to move farther west into a region controlled but seldom traversed by the Spanish. According to Swanton, early in the nineteenth century both the Biloxi and the Pascagoula sold their lands to white planters. Most of them moved to Texas and settled in Angelina County on a bayou named for the Biloxi. Here their earthly course forked. Some returned to spend their last days in Louisiana, but others, probably the majority, moved on into the West and eventually vanished in the Indian melting pot of Oklahoma.

The Biloxi were an irreparably broken tribe, scattered from Avoyelles Parish, Louisiana, to the southern Great Plains. Hodge says that in the early 1800s a few families were still living on Red River, some were "wanderers on Crocodile Bayou," some had found homes with bands belonging to the Caddoan linguistic family, and white traders reported a small Biloxi village on Little River, a tributary of the Brazos River, in Texas. Only about a dozen Biloxi were living in Rapides Parish, Louisiana, in 1892, when Dorsey, recording their language, confirmed the pronouncement of Gatchet, made six years earlier, that they were Sioux.

Soon afterward the last of the Biloxi was gone.

4 The story of the QUAPAW in the South properly, I think, should begin with recorded history, yet scientific investigations have indicated, if not proven, that it may be history which, in fact, has nothing to do with them.

Chroniclers of the De Soto expedition recorded that in the spring of 1541, on the west side of the Mississippi River, near its confluence with the Arkansas, people of a large Indian tribe, called Pacaha and Capaha, were found in a strongly fortified town which was "very great, walled, and beset with towers. . . . Many loopholes were in the towers and wall . . . a great lake came near unto the wall, and it entered into a ditch that went round about the town. . . . From the lake to the great river [Mississippi] was made a weir by which the fish came into it. . . . And in the town was great store of old maize and great quanity of new in the fields. . . . Within a league were great towns, all walled."

These words were written not from field notes but from memory and, as so often occurs, in retrospect scenes change and may present details, dimensions and colors that are exaggerated. Yet, as the ethnologist Cyrus Townsend states, "There are archaeological remains and local conditions in this country [Arkansas] that suit exactly the description of Pacaha . . ." Moreover, this is the same area in which the towns of the Siouan Quapaw stood when Father Marquette, Jolliet, La Salle and other Frenchmen descended the Mississippi more than a century after De Soto.

"The recorded history of the Quapaw," says Townsend, "is commonly supposed to begin with the chronicles of the De Soto expedition," but he was writing at the beginning of this century. Much more information about the subject has since been gained, especially in recent years.

"It was formerly thought," says Swanton, "that the Pacaha or Capaha met by De Soto in this part of Arkansas were the tribe in question [the Quapaw], but it is not probable that they had left the Ohio then, and the name

Capaha, the form on which the relationship is supposed to be established, is probably incorrect." He was writing only some twenty years ago, and in this case the adverb "probably" seems to be superfluous. As cautiousness is an inherent characteristic of all scientists and historians, however, and as Swanton is both and one of the outstanding authorities on Indians, I shall qualify my own following statement regarding the matter.

Although the name *Quapaw* means "downstream people," and *since* there are available old maps and other early documents *purportedly* reflecting the true history of the Quapaw at a time one hundred and fifty years post–De Soto, I suggest it *probably* can be categorically asserted that they were not the Pacaha or Capaha.

It should be noted, however, that some distinguished scholars have advanced the belief that at least some of the Quapaw made their "downstream journey" about the beginning of the sixteenth century. It was postulated by these scientists that perhaps no more than a decade after the first voyage of Columbus the Quapaw began to separate from the other Siouan tribes in the Ohio Valley.

Even if such a contention were correct, the fact remains that both Siouan traditions and historical research indicate that there were Dhegiha Siouans, including Quapaw, in the Ohio Valley considerably more than a hundred years later, and that, in all probability, they abandoned the region to escape the onslaughts of the Iroquois. Their migrations down the Ohio River to the Mississippi unquestionably took place after the Iroquois had obtained guns, for it seems unreasonable to think that all the strong Siouan tribes could have been driven from their ancient homelands by Indians who possessed only conventional prehistoric Indian weapons. The Sioux were capable and courageous warriors.

Linguistically the Quapaw belonged to the Siouan group of tribes to which Dorsey gave the name Dhegiha, which also included the Osage, Omaha, Ponca and Kansa, and possibly the Biloxi. Each of the Dhegiha tribes had a tradition which related that at one time they had lived together or close to each other in the Ohio Valley. They were undoubtedly descendants of the Indian Knoll Siouans, and dwelt in Ohio and southern Indiana on the Wabash River through the periods of the Mound Builder and Hopewell cultures. When they were driven from this region by the Iroquois, they separated at the confluence of the Ohio and Mississippi rivers, some going north and others south.

Besides "downstream people," the name *Quapaw* also signifies "people going with the current." Why they chose to go south, either along or on the Mississippi in dugout canoes, remains a mystery. Perhaps some religious tenet connected with star, moon and sun worship was the basis of their decision. Many Siouan tribes believed that they had lived in the heavens before reaching earth, and even until late in the nineteenth century some of them retained fragments of a tradition of an origin in the Sky World.

The journey going with the current in canoes or larger crafts, such as rafts, could have been accomplished in a few weeks, but the Quapaw did not travel as a tribal unit. Many years passed before the migrations of the 1600s could be considered completed. There were reasons for this: They had no certain location in which they intended to reestablish themselves. They had to be cautious, for they did not know the strange country they were penetrating or what new enemies they might encounter. Each successive group had to sustain itself—whether they were traveling on water or on land they could not carry food supplies sufficient for the entire journey. It was necessary to stop to hunt and to plant crops and harvest them. Children born on the way grew to manhood and womanhood before the trip ended. Moreover, no one was in a hurry.

Sustaining themselves, however, was not a difficult problem. Game, fowl and fish were almost always plentiful, there was an abundance of wild, seasonal, vegetal foods, the land was rich, and the yield of the maize they planted was bountiful. Father Zenobius Membré, who made the same journey a few years later with La Salle, wrote that almost the entire valley of the Mississippi between the Illinois and the Arkansas had delighted every member of the expedition, its beauty and abundance exceeding all their expectations. The swamps and areas in which the great river overflowed were forbidding and unpleasant, but between and behind "these drowned lands you see the finest country in the world . . . there are vast fields of excellent land, diversified here and there with pleasing hills, lofty woods, groves through which you might ride on horseback, so clear and unobstructed are the paths." By the time the Arkansas River and the Quapaw were reached, the "rich, lovely" land knew full spring, and Membré was even more enchanted with it. The air was balmy as the company floated on through the endless twistings of the mighty Father of Waters. Great oaks were adorned with streamers of Spanish moss. The hardwood forests were bright with new foliage. Flowers made colorful palettes of meadows. Birds flashed brilliant plumage among the tall rushes. Alligators sunned themselves on the banks. La Salle's men shot several, finding their meat delectable, and Membré was astonished to learn that the monsters, some of which exceeded twenty feet in length, were born of eggs.

Hyde, an authority on the history of woodland Indians, states that the traditions of the Dhegiha Siouans "indicate an apparently leisurely migration westward and southward." It is his opinion that the "truth probably was that, when attacked, the Siouans deserted their villages and removed to new locations some distance away, where they thought that they would be safe from the Iroquois. When attacked again, they left their new location and moved on. At each move, we may imagine, there were differences of opinion, and part of the people either remained where they were or set off in a chosen direction, leaving the main group behind."

It seems obvious to me that Quapaws—or any other Siouans, for that matter—would follow the course taken previously by members of their own tribe. It must be pointed out, however, that not only Quapaws followed Quapaws. At the time of their migration middle America was a bloody land. The Iroquois did not direct their attacks only against Siouans, but against all Indians. Bands from several linguistic families joined the Quapaws in their southward flight, and the result was a mixture of bloods and of cultures. The pace of the migrations would have been slowed, and the flights would have been spasmodic, for another reason. That is, the Iroquois, powerful as they were, could not maintain a steady pressure—or perhaps they chose to concentrate their aggressions at certain times in other regions—against Midwestern tribes. It is doubtful if they invaded the midlands as often as once a year, and far more likely that their offensives in this area were carried out at intervals of two, or even three, years.

The Algonquians, notably those of the Illinois Confederacy, identified the Ohio Valley Siouans as Akanseas, and called the lower Ohio River on which the Dhegiha tribes lived the Arkansas River. It is from Akansea that the name Kansa came. The Kansa were Dhegiha Sioux. Early French explorers called the Quapaw Akanseas, but did not apply the name to any other Dhegihan tribes.

The first white men known to have met the Quapaw were Père Jacques Marquette and Louis Jolliet and their four companions. After descending the Mississippi from Wisconsin, they found them in 1673 in villages near the mouth of the Arkansas River. It was at this point in their great journey of discovery that Marquette and Jolliet decided to turn back upstream, fearing that they might fall into the hands of the Spanish if they continued. They thought that the Gulf of Mexico was not much farther downstream.

In his brief account of the Quapaw, Marquette makes it clear that while they were permanently established in this area they lived in dire fear of surrounding tribes and were prevented from trading directly with the Spanish by Indian enemies living lower down the river. He found the Quapaw

> very courteous and liberal of what they have, but they are very poorly off for food, not daring to go and hunt the wild cattle [buffalo on the plains to the west]. . . . It is true they have Indian corn in abundance, which they sow at all seasons; we saw some ripe; more just sprouting, and more just in the ear, so that they sow three crops in a year. They cook it in large earthen pots, which are well made; they also have plates of baked earth, which they employ for various purposes.
>
> The men go naked, and wear their hair short; they have the nose and ears pierced, and beads hanging from them. The women are dressed in wretched skins; they braid their hair in two plaits, which falls behind their ears; they have no ornaments to decorate their persons.
>
> Their banquets are without any ceremonies; they serve their meat in large dishes, and everyone eats as much as he pleases, and they give the rest to one another. Their language is extremely difficult. . . . Their cabins, which are long and wide, are made of bark; they sleep at the two extremities, which are raised about two feet from the ground.
>
> They keep their corn in large baskets, made of cane, or in gourds as large as half barrels. They do not know what a beaver is; their riches consisting in the hides of wild cattle. They never see snow, and know the winter only by the rain which falls oftener than in summer. We ate no fruit there but watermelons . . .

If it were true that the Quapaw were prevented by other people from going westward to hunt buffalo on the plains, which seems doubtful, for they would not have had to go very far to find these invaluable animals, they could obtain robes and various other products of the bison from Indian traders, if not on trading missions of their own. Both the lower Mississippi and the Arkansas rivers were major trade arteries. Besides being good farmers, the Quapaw were excellent hunters, and game of all kinds was plentiful in their country. Rivers and lakes supplied them with all the fish they could consume, and they caught them easily in large quantities with nets. Marquette's statement that they were "poorly off for food" seems questionable. Moreover, I think it should be remarked that he had lived in the north, where the finest furs of the continent were to be obtained, and the skins he saw in the hot Southern country may well have appeared "wretched" to him.

Hyde states that "the Indians of this group went on tribal buffalo hunts and grew crops of maize, squash, and beans near their villages ... the only gods among the Quapaws seemed to be earth-bound animals. But they had the calumet ceremony, which indicates a kind of sun worship as well." Marquette also mentions the calumet ceremony. Regarding the disposition of the Quapaws, Hyde says the French were struck by the difference between them and "the silent and rather grim northern tribes, such as the Algonquians." The Quapaws "were good-natured folk, talkative and often laughing and joking." This description of them is supported by other early visitors to the area, one French missionary declaring that the Quapaws were "better made" than Indians of the northern woods, and "civil, liberal, and of a gay humor."

Apparently shortly after Marquette's journey, the Quapaw he met had moved, for a report in Shea (1853) by J. Gavier states that he had camped on the west bank of the Mississippi "half a league from the old village of the Akansea, where they formerly received the late Father Marquette, and which is discernible now only by the old outworks, there being no cabins left." Père Marquette had died in 1675.

Little information about the culture of the Quapaw is provided by archaeological studies, for most materials rapidly deteriorate in the damp climate of their environment. Townsend thinks that the few Quapaw ruins discovered give evidence that they had made a considerable advance in culture, and cites especially their walled towns. He says that they also built "large mounds—the height of one is given as 40 feet—on which they placed, in some instances, their chief buildings." Henri Joutel, a soldier with La Salle, describes a building erected on a mound that was constructed of "great pieces of beautiful cypress wood jointed one with another dovetailed to the top, and covered with bark." He also states that dwellings had "domed roofs," and each accommodated several families.

Townsend quotes one Du Poisson regarding the Quapaws' "painted designs on skin, called *matachee*, which is a skin painted by the Indians with different colors, and on which they paint calumets, birds, and animals. Those of the deer serve as cloths for the table, and those of the buffalo as coverings for the bed." Du Poisson describes the Quapaw ceremonial dress as "well *mataché*, that is having the body entirely painted of different colors, with the tails of wildcats hanging down from places where we usually represent the wings of Mercury, the calumet in their hands, and on their bodies some little bells."

According to Townsend, the Quapaw "method of disposing of their dead was by burial, often in the floor of their houses, though usually they were deposited in graves, sometimes in mounds; sometimes the body was strapped to a stake in a sitting position and then carefully covered with clay." Dorsey was able to obtain the names of seventeen Quapaw gentes, almost all of them named for animals, birds or reptiles. Despite Marquette's statement that "they did not know what a beaver is," the name of one Quapaw gens was *Zhawe*, which means "beaver."

La Salle commanded the second expedition of white men to visit the Quapaw. Late on an afternoon in the spring of 1682, the twelve canoes of his company of thirty-six persons—French Canadian *voyageurs*, a missionary, Indian men and five Indian women—was caught in an impenetrable fog. Through the eerie damp blanket from the right bank of the Mississippi came the sounds of drums and the wild cries of a war dance. Unable to see ahead more than a few yards, they landed on the left bank and quickly erected a defense work of brush and logs.

In the morning the fog lifted and the Quapaw stared across the river at the strange scene. Presently, several warriors cautiously approached in canoes. One of La Salle's Indian companions held aloft a calumet and gave them signs of peace. The warriors landed, and La Salle presented them with tobacco. A Frenchman and two Abnaki Indians returned with them, and soon afterward signaled that they had been well received and that the Quapaw chieftain desired to entertain the visitors.

It is from the chronicles of the La Salle expedition that we obtain an invaluable description of the Quapaw and one of their large villages near the mouth of the Arkansas River.

After receiving the signal from the three emissaries, La Salle and his entire company crossed the river. "The whole village," wrote Father Membré, "came down to the shore to meet us, except the women, who had run off. I cannot tell you the civility and kindness we received from these barbarians, who brought us poles to make huts, supplied us with firewood during the three days we were among them, and took turns in feasting us."

The quiet solemnity of the ceremony La Salle staged was in sharp contrast to the wild dancing with which the Quapaw entertained their guests. They appeared to be entranced by the French ceremony, but they would not have admired and enjoyed it as much if they had understood that it signified the establishment of French rule.

The program was opened by Father Membré. He felt that he had

made a hit with his attempts in the sign language "to explain
something of the truth of God . . ." His audience showed that it
"relished what I said by raising their eyes to heaven, and kneeling as if
to adore."

Next, with La Salle and the famous explorer, Henry de Tonti,
leading them, the Frenchmen marched with dignity to the center of
the village. There a hole was dug, and a tall cross was erected. On it
had been carved the fleur-de-lis. Membré stepped forward and sang a
hymn. To shouts of *vive le roi*, La Salle pronounced the land a
possession of France and all its inhabitants subjects of Louis XIV. The
watching Indians, understanding not a word of what he said, responded with loud applause and cries. Several of them ran forward, giving
signs of their appreciation and, to Membré's great satisfaction,
"rubbed their hands over their bodies after rubbing them over the
cross."

With Quapaw guides, La Salle went on down the river. When he
reached the Taensas, who belonged to the Natchesan linguistic group,
it was learned that they knew more about white men than the
Quapaw, who, presumably, had never previously seen any, except
Marquette and Jolliet. But, said the Taensas, in all the time of the
oldest among them no white man had entered their country. They had
heard that far to the southwest there were bearded white men who
rode great animals, and far to the east and along the great sea there
were others who sailed away to the heavens in ships.

Yet, it was apparent that white men had been in the land of the
Taensas, although they had not ascended the river while the Quapaw
were living at the mouth of the Arkansas. These white men, declared
the Taensas, had been there long before the Quapaw had arrived. La
Salle and his men were shown breastplates of metal and knives and
sabers and buttons and several guns, all made useless by rust, and
they were told that it had come down to them in a legend that at one
time a grand army in armor and plumes and mounted on horses had
passed over the Mississippi and disappeared in the sky. This, of course,
was not a legend. The Taensas were speaking of the army of De Soto
which had passed through their country nearly a century and a half
earlier on its way to disaster.

The Quapaw guides turned back, fearful of encountering enemies of
their tribe, and La Salle drifted on until the Gulf of Mexico had been
reached. The Spanish had found the Mississippi gateway to midland
America, but they had made no effort to hold it. They had established
colonies on each side of it, in Florida and in Texas, but they had failed

to link them together. La Salle had driven, with the force of international law, an indestructible wedge between the two.

The Quapaw, although they did not realize it, in effect had become French subjects in the spring of 1682. Yet, regardless of how much they understood about international politics, before the end of the seventeenth century, they had become firm allies of the French, and this despite the fact that at some time during the last decade of the seventeenth century they were stricken by an epidemic of small pox, and many of them died. One French *voyageur* reported that in two villages the pestilence had destroyed "all the children, and a great part of the women." Whatever may have been the case, because of the disease several of the villages had been abandoned and reestablished in other locations.

Probably during the first quarter of the eighteenth century, the Quapaw moved up the Arkansas River, and settled about twelve miles above the entrance of White River. American soldiers found them in this region shortly after the United States purchased Louisiana Territory. In negotiating with federal officials they asserted territorial claims several hundred miles in length.

The arrival of the Americans marked the beginning of the end for the Quapaw as an individual tribe. Swanton states that by a treaty with the United States "signed at St. Louis, August 24, 1818, they ceded all their claims south of Arkansas River except a small territory between Arkansas Post and Little Rock, extending inland to Saline River." American settlers soon demanded these lands, and the Quapaw gave them up in 1824. They were forced to live in the country of the Caddo Indians, on Bayou Treache on the south side of Red River. This was an area that was often flooded and, therefore, poor farming land—that is why it was assigned to them. The crops they attempted to grow were frequently destroyed, and in the unhealthy environment they suffered from much sickness. They arbitrarily left the region and attempted to establish homes in country on the Arkansas in which they had previously lived.

American settlers protested vigorously that the Quapaw were annoying them, and demanded that they be driven away. Dutifully in 1833 the government reacted by sending the Quapaw to the northeast corner of Indian Territory. Several other treaties were made under which the Quapaw were obliged to move. Most of them finally were permitted to live among the Ponca after 1877. Later they were granted lands in severalty, and eventually became citizens of Oklahoma, but by this time there were not very many of them left.

5   Not many years ago, some archaeologists insisted that the MOSOPELEA were a myth, that no such tribe ever existed and that even if it were possible that some people by this name had existed they certainly did not belong to the Siouan linguistic family.

In supporting such a contention, these scholars were, in effect, asserting that La Salle had swallowed a Seneca fairy tale, that the maps of the earliest French explorers were incorrect, and that such great discoverers as Marquette, Jolliet and Tonti, as well as La Salle, and all the daring missionaries and *voyageurs* who had been members of their expeditions, had made serious mistakes in accounts prepared without a shred of substantiating evidence.

Even as late as 1907, the *Handbook of American Indians*, written by eminent authorities and members of the staff of the American Bureau of Ethnology, stated under the heading *Mosopelea*: "A problematic tribe, first noted on Marquette's map, where *Monsoupelea*, or *Monsouperea*, is marked as an Indian village on the east bank of the Mississippi some distance below the mouth of the Ohio. In 1682 La Salle found a Mosopelea chief with 5 cabins of his people living with the Taensa [on the lower Mississippi], by whom they had been adopted after the destruction of their former village by some unknown enemy." That is the entire content of the statement.

We know now that a tribe called Mosopelea not only existed in prehistoric times, but also played a colorful and dramatic, if relatively unimportant, role in history and were without question a Siouan people.

La Salle did not swallow any fable, but, through no fault of his own, he did make a mistake. On the basis of information he obtained from Senecas, he included the Mosopelea among a list of tribes that were destroyed by the Iroquois. A 1664 map, undoubtedly drawn from La Salle's papers and notes, placed the "destroyed cabins" of the Mosopelea north of the Ohio River in what is now far western Pennsylvania.

The mistake: The village, or villages, of the Mosopelea were destroyed by the Iroquois, but the Mosopelea—probably most of them—escaped and fled westward down the Ohio.

A question that cannot be answered is when the Mosopelea went down the Ohio Valley to escape the Iroquois. Obviously, inasmuch as Marquette located a Mosopelea village on the Mississippi *below* the Ohio in 1673 their southward flight took place before that year. Not far away were camps of Quapaw or Akansea fugitives. In 1682 La Salle found some Mosopelea among the Taensa on the lower Mississippi, and an Akansea chieftain presented him with a Mosopelea youth as a gift. Marquette did not go below the mouth of the Arkansas. The fact suggests that there were Mosopelea among the Akansea [Quapaw] in the years immediately following his visit to the Mississippi-Arkansas confluence.

Adding to the puzzle is the fact that a map drawn by a British mariner, Daniel Coxe, in the early years of the seventeenth century, placed a people he called *Ouesperie* on the north bank of the Ohio River. Coxe had sailed into the lower Mississippi where he obtained considerable information about the location of interior Indian tribes from the French. In his study of the Mosopelea, Swanton declared that the Ouesperie and the Mosopelea were the same people. "Swanton should have added," says Hyde, "that the French had difficulty with the sound of the letter *w* and often substituted *m*, as in *Misconsin* for Wisconsin. At times they used *ou* for *w*, and they often used *b* and *p* interchangeably. This is most important, for it suggests that the Mosopelea were not only Siouan, but probably that group of Siouans who had the name *Wasabe,* meaning *Black Bear.* These Wasabes were still important groups among the five Dhegiha tribes in the nineteenth century, and they were particularly important among the *Osages.*" There are other archaeological sites in the Memphis area, on the Mississippi both above and below the metropolis, that are believed by some scientists to have been Mosopelea towns. The Mosopelea, in all probability, were one of the smaller Siouan groups, and the evidence presented above indicates that their migration from their earliest known homeland on the Allegheny or upper Ohio rivers continued over many years, at least approximately from 1670 to 1700.

The name Mosopelea probably came from an Algonquian dialect, but its meaning is uncertain, and how they got it is not known. They identified themselves by the name *Ofo*. This may be an abbreviation of a Muskhogean language term, *Ofogoula*, meaning "Ofo people," but it also can be interpreted, according to Swanton, as "Dog People." In fact, the Mosopelea were called Dog People by a number of other tribes, but the reason why this appellation was applied to them has not been discovered. Perhaps they owned a large number of dogs, and considered puppies a delicacy in the stew pot. In any case, I think that they might well have been called *Stray Dog People*, for from the time Europeans first heard of them until they disappeared from the earth they were itinerants.

It cannot be said where they dwelt before they came onto the historical stage in Ohio, although nothing has come to light to indicate that what little is known of Sioux origins is not applicable to them as much as any other Siouan group. But their story as we know it belongs entirely to the historical period and, as will be seen, no one deserves more the right to complete that story than the famed ethnologist, linguist and Indian historian, John R. Swanton.

These are his words:

> . . . they appear to have stopped for a time among the Quapaw, but before 1686 at least part of them had sought refuge among the Taensa. Their reason for leaving the latter tribe is unknown, but Iberville found them on the lower Yazoo River, close to the Yazoo and Koroa Indians. . . . When their neighbors, the Yazoo and Koroa, joined in the Natchez uprising [1729], the Ofo [Mosopelea] refused to side with them and went to live with the Tunica, who were French allies. Shortly before 1739 they had settled close to Fort Rosalie [in the country of the Natchez on the lower Mississippi], where they remained until 1758. In 1784 their village was on the Western bank of the Mississippi 8 miles above Point Coupee [Louisiana].
>
> *But nothing more was heard of them until 1908, when I found a single survivor living among the Tunica just out of Marksville, La., and was able to establish their linguistic connections.*

⑥ The PASCAGOULA were so closely associated with the Biloxi that there is no reason to think that they were not a Siouan group. Except for the fact that the Pascagoula are believed to have been living on the river named for them when the Biloxi migrated southward from the Ohio Valley, the history of the two tribes is almost identical.

In the respect that they are always mentioned in connection with the Biloxi, the same statement might be made of the Moctobi. Indeed, some ethnologists are convinced that the Moctobi were a subdivision of the Biloxi.

The first known historical mention of the Pascagoula was made by Iberville. He reported hearing their name when he landed in Mobile Bay in 1699. In the summer of the same year his brother, Bienville, found them living in three villages on the Pascagoula River about twelve leagues above its mouth in what is now southern Mississippi. Other Frenchmen visited the Pascagoula, presumably to establish trade relations with them, in the spring of 1700.

Not all scientists agree that the Pascagoula were Siouans, some preferring to believe that originally they were Muskhogeans, but no one disputes that at least from the year 1699 through much of the nineteenth century they were intimately associated and intermarried with the Biloxi. The disagreement, however, is largely based on the slim evidence that the name Pascagoula means "Bread People" in the language of the Muskhogean Choctaw. It should be noted that the names by which numerous tribes are known to history derive from tongues they did not speak. No vocabulary of the Pascagoula's language has been preserved. Even the name by which they identified themselves has not survived.

Only a very few Pascagoula were still living in Louisiana as late as the early years of the nineteenth century. All the others—an unknown number—were the Biloxi (q.v.). Following completion of his studies of the Southern Siouans, early in this century, Swanton reported: "I have been able to find no Indians in Louisiana claiming Pascagoula descent, but in 1914 there were two among the Alabama who stated that their mother was of this tribe, their father having been a Biloxi." There seems to be no doubt that almost all of the Pascagoula—although at one time they resided in villages of their own—eventually became incorporated with the Biloxi.

If the Moctobi spoke a different dialect of the Siouan language than the Biloxi, linguists have not been able to gain such knowledge. In connection with the Biloxi and Pascagoula, Iberville did speak of a small tribe he called *Capinans*, and they appeared on a 1707 French map by this name; there seems to be no question but that they were identical with the Moctobi.

At the beginning of this century the Bureau of American Ethnology stated: "The name Moctobi appears to have disappeared from Indian memory and tradition . . ."

If repeated inquiries in subsequent years failed to find any trace of it, there is, indeed, little chance that it will ever reappear.

7   All Southern Siouan tribes were relatively small. It is
doubtful if their total population at the beginning of the
historical period exceeded 5,000 men, women and children.

Also, there are very few Southern Siouan place names to
be found on today's maps. Those existing are:

TRIBE	PLACE NAME
Quapaw	Village in Oklahoma, Arkansas River, Arkansas State, Arkansas County, Arkansas City and Arkansas Post, in Arkansas. Arkansas City, Kansas. Arkansas (town), Wisconsin.
Pascagoula	River, city and bay in Mississippi.
Biloxi	City and bay in Mississippi.

The names of the Mosopelea and the Moctobi have not
been preserved in place names.

PART FOUR

The Sioux of the Midwestern Prairies and Middle Great Plains

1 The origin myths of the Dhegiha and Chiwere divisions of the Siouan linguistic family are no less wondrous and imaginative than the Biblical story of Creation.

The Osage, Omaha, Ponca and Kansa, who spoke Dhegiha dialects, and the Iowa, Missouri and Oto, who belonged to the Chiwere branch, tell in religious myths of their origins in the sky. This Upper World was divided into three parts, or layers, one above the other.

Underhill cites as an example of this creation myth a ritual of the Osage Black Bear Clan which describes "the descent of these pre-human spirits as they floated down from the topmost of the layered worlds." After making "downward soarings" through all three of the Upper Worlds, they "came to the earth, which lay engulfed in water.* They alighted on seven rocks of different colors . . ." None of the earth creatures they met could help them over the water that submerged the earth. "Finally the Great Elk appeared and

Threw himself suddenly upon the water,
And the dark soil of the earth
He made to appear by his strokes.†

"With four of these tremendous movements," Underhill adds, "he cleared away the water . . ." Thus, the Great Elk gave the people "dry land for their dwelling. He then bade them take the various-colored soils, which his hooves had thrown up, to paint their faces in time of war. Even the seeds of corn, in the myths of the Omaha and Osage, were provided by the elk or the buffalo."

While origin myths of the tribes contained variations in their telling, and some tribes revered more supernaturals than others, all thought of themselves as being inextricably

*This factor is contained in origin myths in many parts of the world.
†Underhill quoting from La Flesche.

woven into the natural scheme of the universe as they conceived it. They were not simply pieces of bone and flesh, not simply possessors of certain faculties. They were those things, but they were also of the sky and the earth, of the elements and the animals, of the plants and grasses and trees—of everything that existed and of everything that was born and lived and died in the eternal cycle of life.

Some scholars suggest that the Sioux recognized a *Supreme Power of Creation*, rather than a *Supreme Being*, such as the Christian God. Other students of Siouan religion state that the Sioux believed in a personalized yet *Universal Power* which governed their every act. The latter concede that this quality of deity may have been influenced to some extent by the long contacts of their informants with missionaries and other whites. However, they point out that Siouan religious authorities they consulted, many of whom had not been converted to Christian faiths, maintained that the native religion of the Siouan people embraced a belief in a *Supreme Supernatural* possessed of *Divine Power*.

The beliefs of most Siouan tribes or divisions did not include a conception of a hereafter that might be likened to the Christian Heaven and Hell. Their ritual in its system of imitative and sympathetic magic was aimed almost in its entirety at fulfillment of the requirements of life and living. The Teton and the Winnebago, however, were notable exceptions, both being profoundly concerned with what they thought of as a *last hunting ground*.

Speaking generally, it is improbable that any people on earth were more influenced by the supernatural, or more guided by spiritual beliefs, than the Indian. Unlike white society, which tends to turn religion on and off as needs demand and moods please, the primitive Indian was never detached from it, day or night. It affected very nearly everything he did and everything he thought.

"It is difficult," says Lowie, "to separate faith from observance, for the native who believes in supernatural beings will try to placate them by some act; and if he thinks that a certain procedure would bring rain or any other desired end, he will apply it."

Driver states: "Gods, ghosts, and other spirits are supposed to have intelligence, emotions, and free will comparable to those of men. They may intervene in the affairs of the world and of man in a manner consistent with a system of ethics or according to their whims of the moment. . . . They may be benevolent, malevolent, or merely unconcerned, but they are generally susceptible to human pleading and bend an ear to prayers, sacrifices, and other forms of emotional appeal to their egos."

Worship was not always expressed through group ceremonials. A man might have a totem sacred to him alone in his own thoughts, painted on his shield or even tattooed on his skin. He might seek to appease a supernatural by cleansing his body. Invariably, he would go alone into the wilderness to fast and pray. And, above all, he would hope for a vision, or revelation, from a spirit in answer to some desire, to cure an affliction, to instill bravery, to bring him success in life.

Religion was not a thing apart from other phases of life. It permeated every act—in planting, in warfare, in conception, in hunting and even in death. The Siouans carried their forms of the Mound Builder culture with them to the midland prairies west of the Mississippi, and to the woodlands west of the Great Lakes. The effigy-type mound was predominent in the northern part of this region. The sites of hundreds of mounds of many types have been located by archaeologists in Missouri, Iowa, Kansas, Nebraska, Wisconsin and Minnesota.

The spirits were never idle, and always they were watching the people they had created and sent to live on earth.

2   The Sioux of the prairies west of the Mississippi and the middle Great Plains probably did not acquire horses in any appreciable numbers until late in the seventeenth century. Before this time some of them undoubtedly had obtained firearms from French traders.

Nothing caused greater changes in the way of life of both the Midwestern and the Northern Sioux than the horse and the gun. The dispersion of the horse was from south to north, but the gun reached the Sioux from three directions, east, north and south.

The northern spread of the horse from Mexico, where it had been introduced and bred by the Spanish, was exceedingly swift. Twenty or thirty years before 1600 northern Mexican and western Texas tribes were raiding each other to obtain them. So rapidly did the number of horses increase that by the beginning of the seventeenth century these Indians could obtain horses in another way besides stealing them from the Spanish or each other. According to one contemporary report, there were large numbers of them grazing on the vast ranges, "so many that they go wild in the country, without owner, which ones are called *cimarrones* . . . some that live all their lives without an owner." Haines states that horses had reached western Nebraska as early as 1720, eastern Kansas and western Missouri by 1724, Montana by 1730, and the northern Great Plains by 1750. These may be conservative estimates by a cautious scholar but, in any case, they mean that the Sioux were in possession of horses by these dates.

There is documentary evidence to show that the seventeenth century was not very old when the Spanish gave up their attempts to prevent Indians from acquiring horses. The situation was far beyond possible control, and they concentrated their efforts on the more important task of staying alive under the burden of almost constant raids against them by mounted Indians.

Actually, the Spanish were themselves responsible, in certain ways, for the rapidity with which the horse reached the Midwestern plains and prairies. As they continued to push northward—not only treasure hunters but trading expeditions as well—each year they abandoned more mounts or lost them in stampedes caused by buffalo, cougars, wolves and marauding Indians. Perhaps before 1650, and undoubtedly in the next two decades, Spanish expeditions of various types had traveled north of the Platte River, and there is information indicating that a hundred and fifty years before the Lewis and Clark expedition Spanish traders had ridden northward along the eastern base of the Rocky Mountains as far as southern Montana. There, among the Kiowas, they saw horses, but not very many. However, within another twenty years other people of the northern area also had become mounted Indians.

It seems reasonable to assume that the Sioux, as did most other people of the West and Midwest, realized the power, value and usefulness of guns and horses long before they had acquired them. They were prizes which all Siouans strived for strenuously, and not infrequently engaged in bloody conflict, to obtain. One of the greatest triumphs a young warrior ~ould achieve was the theft of horses belonging to any enemy. No Indians were more skillful at stealing horses than the Sioux.

Although the gun in some areas reached the Sioux in quantity before the horse, and in other areas at a later period, its adoption, for obvious reasons, followed at a slower pace. All lead and powder had to be obtained from white men. A gun without them was not as good a weapon as a war club with a flint spike in it. Guns could be stolen or captured, but obtaining sufficient supplies of powder and lead was extremely difficult. Moreover, a single-shot gun could not be loaded and fired as rapidly as arrows. Even long after Americans had begun to push westward from the Mississippi, the Sioux and other western Indians continued to fight with their traditional weapons, the lance, the bow and arrow, the hatchet and the club, both in intertribal conflicts and against the destroyers of their hunting grounds. Thus, it was the cartridge and the repeating rifle that contributed greatly to the destruction of the Indians. By the time they acquired this deadly weapon they were nearing the end of their tether.

It should be stated, as well, that solving the mechanics of the musket and developing skill in using them were not easily accomplished. The horse was easier to understand and to use. It was an animal. It ate grass, and it left droppings, and its meat was edible (although the Sioux did not eat horsemeat, except in times of great hunger that could not be assuaged by other food), and it propagated and took care of itself. No explosive and fire were needed to make it operate. The horse made it possible to travel long distances in commerce and war. It allowed the Indian to increase the quantity of his personal possessions. A pack pony could pull a travois loaded with a large tepee, robes, utensils and foodstuffs, and at the same time could carry a squaw and several papooses. On trading missions or journeys to councils and ceremonies, this incomparably strong beast of burden could travel from dawn until dark with a heavy load of commodities or a rider, and in the evening it would roll and drink and refresh itself on grass. The advantages which it provided in hunting are apparent.

The prairies and plains of the Sioux Country were a natural home for the horse. The grass was nutritious and dependable. If this fine fodder failed or was destroyed by fire in one place, it could usually be found growing in other places not far distant. Instinctively the horse moved, like the buffalo, to find its food. Carnivorous enemies took a relatively small toll of the horse, for it was intelligent and swift, both means of self-protection, and when cornered was a vicious fighter.

The horse was a cultural force with which, as far as the Sioux are concerned, no instrument invented by man may be equated, not even the gun. The gun, of course, because of the many drastic changes that can be attributed to it, ranked second. It made hunting easier and, when it could be properly used, it provided an incomparable power in both defensive and offensive warfare.

Together, therefore, the horse and the gun transformed Stone Age Sioux warriors—almost overnight, one might say—into formidable and skillful fighters and raiders, indeed, unsurpassed in these respects by any other Western Indians who fought valiantly in defense of their traditional homelands.

3 The first known historical homes west of the Mississippi of the seven Siouan tribes of the Midwestern prairies and middle plains were:

IOWA: On the Upper Iowa River, in the State of Iowa.

MISSOURI: On the Missouri River near the mouth of Grand River, in the state of Missouri.

OSAGE: The largest branch, called Great Osage, on Osage River, and another branch, called Little Osage, on the Missouri River near the Missouri Indians, both locations in the state of Missouri.

OMAHA: On the Missouri River in northeastern Nebraska.

OTO: On the lower Platte River in the state of Nebraska.

PONCA: At the confluence of Missouri and Niobrara rivers, in the state of Nebraska.

KANSA: On the Kansas River in eastern part of the state of Kansas.

4   They were people of the Middle Mississippi Culture, and they were cannibals. In a place called American Bottom, on the east side of the Mississippi across the river from St. Louis, they built the great Cahokia Mound, the largest prehistoric manmade earth structure in the world.

The Illinois period of the Middle Mississippi Culture is dated A.D. 1300–1600 by archaeologists. At some time in the sixteenth century a part of these Indians of Cahokia moved northward into south-central Wisconsin. On a tributary of Rock River (in Jefferson County) they built a large fortified town, Aztalan. It was in this region that they came into contact with the Chiwere Siouans. The Iowa, Oto and Missouri were then in close association with the Winnebago, who are sometimes referred to as the "mother group" of this linguistic division. There is nothing to suggest, however, where any of these Chiwere tribes had previously resided, what routes they had followed to reach the Wisconsin area or how long they had occupied it when the Cahokians arrived.

According to various scholars, the walls of Aztalan enclosed about seventeen acres, a very large space for any prehistoric Indian town. Martin, Quimby and Collier state that Aztalan was "well protected by a palisade of upright logs covered with clay and grass. At frequent intervals along the stockade there were square towers. Within the palisade there were large, flat-topped pyramidal mounds of earth upon which wooden temples of chiefs' houses were built. These pyramids were arranged around a central plaza." Noting that the Aztalan were farmers and consumed wild game, fowl and fish, these authorities add, "There is evidence that the diet of the Aztalan Indians included human flesh. Human bones, many cracked for the marrow, were found in refuse pits along with animal bones . . ."

"At Aztalan and also in village ruins of the same culture and period near the mouth of the Wisconsin River," Hyde says,

> there are clear indications of cannibalism. Archaeology has record-
> ed this fact and let it go at that; but to the historian the
> cannibalism of the Aztalan . . . is another matter that connects
> these southern Indians with the Winnebago Siouans of Wisconsin,
> who, from about the year 1640 on, were described by the French as
> notorious cannibals. The district on the Mississippi in south-
> western Wisconsin and across the river in northeastern Iowa and
> southeastern Minnesota is believed to have been held by the Iowas
> and Otoes . . . and since cannibalistic evidence was found in this
> area, it seems a fair inference that the Siouans of the Winnebago
> group were infected with the habit of eating human flesh by the
> Aztalan Indians, with whom they were living and whom they
> admired because of their higher culture.

The comparatively small region about the confluence of the Missis-sippi and Wisconsin rivers seems to mark the end of the trail of Siouan cannibalism. Archaeology has not produced evidence to show that the degenerate practice was carried farther westward by any Siouan tribe.

The Aztalan were competent craftsmen, and manufactured beau-tiful gorgets, beads and other ornaments of copper obtained from the veins near Lake Superior. They also made beads, pendants and other jewelry from shells that reached them over the Mississippi River trade route from the Gulf of Mexico. Apparently, this highly developed Middle Mississippi Culture had a magnetic influence on the Siouans, whose way of life was, by comparison, extremely crude, and they flocked to Aztalan and established themselves in adjoining villages.

If by nothing else, such a conclusion is substantiated by the pottery found in the Aztalan ruins and the immediately adjacent area. Some of the ceramics are of the old Cahokia type, some are Siouan of the Effigy Mound period, and some contain features of both of these types. Hyde expresses the opinion that "from this mingling at Aztalan—and apparently at other Cahokian centers on the Mississippi near the mouth of the Wisconsin—developed the next phase of Siouan culture in the upper Mississippi Valley, which is termed Oneota."

Speaking of the Oneota aspect as a major culture, which may be characterized as a prairie entity, Wedel states that "Oneota materials occur principally in Iowa, southern Minnesota, Wisconsin, Illinois and Missouri." Martin, Quimby and Collier give a date of A.D. 1400–1700 for the Oneota Culture, and conjecture that "the presence of European trade material in some Oneota sites indicates a later period for this culture. Early Oneota seems to antedate White contact in certain areas. The Oneota Indians have been identified with the Winnebago in Wisconsin, the Iowa and Oto in Iowa, the Oto in Nebraska, and the Missouris in Missouri . . ." They also make the important statement that "the culture of the Oneota Indians has southern as well as northern affinities. Probably it represents a blending of southern and northern cultures which produced a new hybrid related to both yet distinguishable from either."

How long Aztalan existed is questionable, and there is a sharp difference of opinion among scientists. In any case, it was not a peaceful period, for, being cannibals and craving material treasures, the Aztalans raided tribes to the north, east and west to obtain victims for their grizzly feasts and materials and goods they desired. Siouans who refused to become allied with them were attacked by their war parties and engaged in bloody fighting with them. Moreover, some Siouan groups violently disapproved of their cannibalism and the male homosexualism that was widespread among them. Early records indicate that the Winnebago acquired the sexual vice from them, but there is no evidence to show that it became common as a result of the Aztalan influence among other Chiwere Siouan tribes.

It is probable that Aztalan's end came about 1600, or perhaps a few years later. Some archaeologists believe it might have been inhabited as late as the 1630s. The fact remains that the Aztalan abandoned their great town, and fled southward down the Mississippi, most likely to their former home at Cahokia. Aztalan was destroyed, largely by fire, but who set the conflagration is not known.

Archaeologists have been unable to determine the cause of the flight of the Aztalan, but two beliefs are advanced: (1) that they departed hurriedly when they feared an attack on them was imminent by Indians from the north and northeast who had acquired firearms from white men; or (2) they were actually attacked and driven out by superior forces.

Of one thing there can be no doubt. At the beginning of the seventeenth century all Indians of the Great Lakes and upper Mississippi regions knew that white men were pushing steadily westward from the St. Lawrence Valley. The historical period had begun for them.

5   If a Siouan tradition that was related as late as the nineteenth century can be believed, the IOWA were the first Chiwere people to leave the Aztalan region and move westward to the Mississippi River where the states of Wisconsin, Iowa and Minnesota touch each other. This migration took place in the first half of the seventeenth century, most probably in the early part of this period.

It is quite possible, however, that at least three other Siouan groups moved westward across the Mississippi from the Winnebago area much earlier. Hyde states that archaeological evidence indicates that "part of the Winnebago [Chiwere] group had a great center of population near the mouth of the Wisconsin, and across the Mississippi in northeastern Iowa, in the Effigy Mound period, which is earlier than the Aztalan period." He thinks that besides the Iowa, Oto and Missouri, the "old Winnebago group" also probably included "the Mandans, Hidatsas, and Crows," and that some of these people evidently migrated to and beyond the Mississippi in Effigy Mound times. "Of these movements we have no traditional accounts," he points out, "and the evidence of archaeology is scanty. It may be observed, however, that the Hidatsas and Crows seem to have taken Effigy Mound culture with them on their westward and northward migration . . ." The Hidatsa and Mandan eventually established themselves on the upper Missouri River, and the Crow settled in southern Montana.

The Iowa have a tradition of having dwelt in a large fortified town, probably Aztalan, with the Oto, Missouri and Winnebago. Why they moved westward is uncertain, but at the time of their migration, indeed throughout most of the first half of the seventeenth century, the Great Lakes region was aflame with intertribal warfare.

There is some controversy over the origin and meaning of the word *Iowa*. Swanton suggests that apparently it was borrowed by early French traders or missionaries from

Ayuhwa, a term applied to the tribe by the Dakota Sioux. Riggs interprets *Ayuhwa* as "sleepy ones." Skinner declares that *Iowa* is their own name. Dorsey states, and Swanton agrees, that they identify themselves by the name *Pahodja,* and that it is their own name. Dorsey translates *Pahodja* as "dusty noses." Hyde says that their native name was *Paoutet,* and that at one time they were called "dusty ones."

The Iowa are not known to have performed any feats of great significance and certainly they were not exceedingly conspicuous as a tribal entity. From the early reports of white explorers, traders and missionaries, it may be deduced that they were unenterprising and somewhat indifferent as hunters and cultivators. In their geographical position—that is, adjacent to tribes of the Great Plains—they became influenced to some extent by plains customs, but they remained intermediate between Woodland and Plains people. Lowie notes that "they surrounded buffalo, dressed skins with elk-horn scrapers, crossed rivers in bull boats, traveled with travois, and had rival military clubs." These were customs of some true Plains Indians. But the Iowa never became "pure hunters." They made wooden utensils and pottery, planted crops of corn, beans and squash, and played lacrosse, a game characteristic of the eastern United States. Also, the Iowa—and this was true of the Oto, Missouri and other Siouan tribes of the region treated in this part—had the same patrilineal clan organization of such true Woodland Indians as the Winnebago and the Algonquians.

The French explorer, Radisson, may have been the first white man to encounter the Iowa. He claimed that he found them on the Mississippi River in 1655. The exact location is in doubt, but it is believed to be above the Iowa River's mouth. Some authorities believe that in the earliest historical period, which would be at the time of Radisson's explorations in the area, if, in fact, he reached it, the Iowa were living on the upper Iowa River. However, ruins have been found along this section of the Mississippi that unquestionably were originally Iowa or Oto villages.

The Iowa are known to have moved frequently after the beginning of the historical period. Swanton traces their migrations in more or less chronological order to the northwest part of Iowa State, about the Okoboji Lakes, to southwestern Minnesota, and to the Big Sioux River. In the latter part of the eighteenth century, he states, they were on the Missouri River near Council Bluffs. A few years later they were on the Des Moines River. Here the tribe apparently separated—at least temporarily—some going to live on the Grand River in Missouri. At some time in their wanderings during the early years of the nineteenth century they ran into a band of Dakota Sioux who evidently did not welcome their presence and blood was shed. There is a tradition that in 1821 they were attacked and defeated by Sauk and Fox warriors led by the famous chief Black Hawk.

By a series of treaties "negotiated" between 1824 and 1837 the Iowa relinquished all territorial claims in the states of Iowa, Minnesota and Missouri. They were assigned a reservation that included lands along the Great Nemaha River in Kansas and Nebraska, but white farmers soon wanted this rich region, and the Iowa were ousted and sent to Oklahoma. Eventually they were granted lands in severalty, but by this time there were not many survivors.

As they were relatively inconspicuous in early historical times, the numerous ways in which the name Iowa is preserved seems unwarranted, but they do have one genuine claim to distinction.

On the western slope of the Coteau des Prairie, the divide between the drainages of the Mississippi and Missouri rivers, in southwestern Minnesota, is one of the most famous Indian sites in America. It is the Red Pipestone Quarry. Through centuries it played an important part in the religious, social and economic cultures of virtually every tribe that inhabited the middle and northern woodlands, prairies and plains. Since 1937 it has been a national monument.

The country of the Pipestone area is gently rolling. Outcroppings of quartzite bedrock frequently occur, and between the layers of these deposits is a red claystone. It is a fine-grained argillaceous sediment, and when freshly quarried is so soft that it may be easily carved with stone knives and drilled with primitive hand drills. From this material thousands of pipes of innumerable sizes and types, and for use in countless ceremonies, rituals and councils, have been made by Indian artisans and, indeed, are still being made.

Siouans occupied the Coteau des Prairie in late prehistoric times— the Mandan may have been the first Siouan tribe to live at Pipestone, which is on a small affluent of the Big Sioux River—and controlled it until the end of tribal days. To them it was always a sacred place, a shrine, but they did not overlook its value as a stimulant to their economy.

When he visited Pipestone in 1836, the famous painter of Indians, George Catlin, recorded a tradition related by Siouans he met there. "Many ages after the red men were made," Catlin was told,

when all the different tribes were at war, the Great Spirit sent
runners and called them all together at the Red Pipe. He stood on
the top of the rocks, and the red people were assembled in infinite
numbers on the plains below. He took out of the rock a piece of the
red stone and made a large pipe; he smoked it over them all; told
them that it was part of their flesh; that though they were at war,
they must meet at this place as friends; that it belonged to them
all; that they must make their calumets [pipes] from it and smoke
them to him whenever they wished to appease him or get his
good-will—the smoke from his big pipe rolled over them all, and he
disappeared in its cloud; at the last whiff of his pipe a blaze of fire
rolled over the rocks, and melted their surface—at that moment
two squaws went in a blaze of fire under the two medicine rocks,
where they remain to this day, and must be consulted and
propitiated whenever the pipestone is to be taken away.

Although many white men had been at the quarry during the
century preceding Catlin's visit, he was the first to inform mineralo-
gists of the peculiar soft stone, and they named it Catlinite.

It is believed by archaeologists that the first quarrying at Pipestone
was done by the Iowa in the early 1600s. The Oto may have been with
them. In any case, whether they must share it or not, it is the Iowa's
only claim to fame.

Long before French *voyageurs* met the OTO, and for many years after the beginning of the American period of western expansion, they were so closely associated with the Iowa that in many respects the history of the two tribes is almost identical. The same statement may be made with regard to their ways of life and their spiritual beliefs.

If the westward migrations of the Oto and Iowa did not occur simultaneously, they were separated by only a short period of time. Winnebago traditions relate that the Iowa left them before the Oto, but even if that is correct it does not signify that the Oto moved out of the Aztalan area at a much later date than the Iowa. Actually, the opposite appears to be the case. Archaeological sites of the Oneota Culture along the Mississippi, in Iowa and southern Minnesota bespeak the presence of both tribes in this region in the first half of the seventeenth century.

According to Swanton, the Oto's own name was *Che-wae-rae*, and *Oto* comes from the word *Wat'ota*, which means "lechers."

This derogatory name, by which they have become known in history, apparently was inflicted on them some years after they crossed the Mississippi and at a time when they were moving southwestward in north-central Missouri. The exact year is not known.

When explorers and missionaries first reached the lower Missouri River they were told a tale by aged Oto chiefs. At least in part, it must be classed as a tradition, but modern-day research suggests that it is rooted in some reality.

The tale was this: At some time, two tribes, the Missouri and the Oto, were traveling together when they came to the confluence of the Missouri and Grand rivers. There a breach was created between them that was never healed. The row reportedly occurred when the son of the Oto chief raped, or at least seduced, a daughter of the Missouri chief. So great was the anger of the girl's father that he called the entire tribe of the young seducer *Wat'ota*, and led his own people away from them. The Oto were never able to escape the approbrium fastened upon them in this incident.

Like other Chiwere tribes, the Oto participated in building effigy mounds and carried this culture with them west of the Mississippi. They have a tradition of having lived in or near a great fortified town with the Iowa and Missouri, which may have been Aztalan, but if at one time they ate human flesh they left the practice behind them when they moved west of the Mississippi. Although it appears that they seldom lived very far from the Iowa, the Oto seem to have preferred to stay in villages exclusively their own. Habitually the Oto built permanent earthen dwellings, identical with those of other Siouan tribes of the region, but apparently they were not permanent occupants of them. They were cultivators, but cannot be called farmers in the fullest sense of the word. They adopted characteristics of the Middle Plains cultures, while retaining much of their old Woodland culture.

The Oto moved frequently (as did the Iowa), and Hyde attributes their shiftings to the invasion of their lands by Algonquians who were driven west of the Mississippi by the Iroquois. However, I believe another element should be injected into this contention, that of a peculiar restlessness with which the Oto seem to have been imbued. They obviously wandered on long forays and hunts across the Great Plains, and although they planted some crops and established villages, instead of terming them a semisedentary people it may be more appropriate to describe them as roamers and hunters. They certainly fell into this category in the early historical period. An event which occurred in 1680 serves as an illustration. In that year a contingent of Oto visited La Salle on the Illinois River. They were on foot, but they told him they had traveled far enough west to get in a fight with white bearded men who rode horses, unquestionably Spaniards in the western parts of Nebraska or Kansas, and possibly in eastern Colorado. Their own village, they informed La Salle, was five days west of his fort near Peoria, Illinois, and in their westward journeys, after traveling only five days beyond their homes they had seen mounted Indians. Hyde notes that one Oto chief of this party had a horse hoof tied to his belt as a trophy.

As far as is known, the company of French traders led by Radisson were the first white men to meet the Oto. This event occurred in 1655 on the Mississippi, at some location above the mouth of the Wisconsin.

The Iowa were nearby. Hyde thinks that these two tribes must have been living in permanent villages at the time, "for they had a big supply of maize, enough to trade to Radisson's party of over 150 persons all the maize needed for the rest of the journey up the river."

A 1673 map of Père Marquette places the Oto on the Des Moines River. The Iowa were not far away, to the north. In 1700 traders found them on the Blue Earth River, again near the Iowa. During the next century they moved a number of times, both in Iowa and Missouri, but there is controversy over their locations, traditions and reports conflicting to the extent that it is extremely difficult, if not impossible, to ascertain their whereabouts at any given time.

About the end of the eighteenth century, however, it is definitely known that they were on the Missouri River, and by 1804 they had established themselves on the Platte River not far from its confluence with the Missouri, where they lived for a number of years.

Several treaties resulted in their giving up all their lands. First they relinquished their territorial claims in Missouri and Iowa. They managed to hold on to some lands in Kansas and Nebraska as late as 1881, then agreed to live on a reservation to be selected for them by the federal government. They were sent to Oklahoma.

The Oto were always a small tribe, and they were never known to be warlike. This may account for the fact that a large proportion of them survived when other tribes were all but wiped out by American settlers and soldiers. Most of their descendants, numbering several hundred, still live in Oklahoma, citizens of that state. All the Missouri, who allegedly fastened on them the defamatory name, have been long gone.

7   Judging from the widespread use of the word MISSOURI, one might be inclined to think that the Chiwere Siouan tribe bearing this name held high rank in the Indian history of the American Midwest. That would be a mistake. The Missouri were a small, unimportant and undistinguished group and, as Swanton states, their name "has attained a distinction out of all proportion to the aboriginal standing of the people."

Their own name was *Niutachi*, and its meaning is uncertain. Nor is it known whether the Missouri River was named for them or they were called the Missouri simply because they dwelt on the great river when white men first met them. The word *missouri* does not come from the Siouan tongue. It derives from the Illini dialect of the Algonquian language. In early historical times it was erroneously interpreted as "big muddy," and this popular nickname for the Missouri River still prevails but, actually, it signifies "people having dugout canoes."

There seems to be no question that the Missouri left the Winnebago area of Wisconsin and migrated westward across the Mississippi in close association with the Iowa and Oto. The Iowa remained in present Iowa State, but the Oto and Missouri—or at least some groups of them—continued on to the Missouri River. The bitter quarrel between the Oto and Missouri at the conjunction of the Missouri and Grand rivers has been recounted in the previous chapter.

The culture of the Missouri, while always retaining woodland traits, was in the historical period strongly oriented to the ways of life of plains tribes. Wedel states that the "villages of the Missouri, since their first recorded notice in 1673 [by Père Marquette], were along or near the Missouri River, below the mouth of the Kansas. Most of these locations have been verified by archaeology. . . . There is no trace of earth lodges, but good evidence that the subsistence economy included agriculture, hunting, fishing, and gathering. The pottery . . . is mostly of the Oneota type." One of the most productive archaeological locations was found near a place called The Pinnacles, in Saline County, Missouri, a few miles above the mouth of the Grand River.

It is believed that the Missouri remained at The Pinnacles until 1798, when they were attacked by the Sauk and Fox. Many of them were slain, and the survivors scattered among the Osage, Kansa and Oto. During the next seven years the refugees gradually reunited, and Lewis and Clark found them south of the River Platte. According to Swanton, as the result of "another unfortunate war, this time with the Osage, part joined the Iowa but the greater part went to the Oto to live, and followed their fortunes, participating with them in all treaties onward."*

Only thirteen persons of the Missouri blood were reported to be alive by the United States Census of 1910.

*See previous chapter.

8   In August, 1601, somewhere on the plains along the Arkansas River, in what is now central Kansas, Spanish treasure hunters commanded by Governor Juan de Oñate of New Mexico met some Indians to whom they gave the name of *Escanjaques.* The identity of these people never has been conclusively established, and most probably never will be, but the location of the meeting has prompted some scholars to suggest that they may have been the KANSA. If that were true, it would mean that the historical period began for this Siouan tribe in the second year of the seventeenth century. Recent research, however, seems to prove beyond any doubt that the conjecture is totally unacceptable.

The identities of the first white men to encounter the Kansa are unknown. The most reasonable assumption, in the view of this author, is that French *voyageurs*, whose names are lost to history, met them somewhere on the Missouri River. A French map, purportedly drawn in 1674 under the direction of Marquette, places them on the Kansas River. This location was furnished the missionary by someone else, for he did not meet the Kansa. Another French record, dated half a century earlier, notes that a large village of the Kansa stood on a "small river flowing from the north 30 leagues above Kansas River and near the Missouri." According to Wedel, the Fanning archaeological site, in extreme northeastern Kansas (Doniphan County), "has yielded small metal items and glass beads in some quantity; it was very likely inhabited between 1650 and 1700, roughly speaking; and it is in or near the locality where the Kansas were presumably living at about that time."

There is nothing to indicate that the Dhegiha Siouan division, to which the Kansa belong, migrated westward from the Ohio Valley region in a mass movement. However, there is circumstantial evidence suggesting that the migrations took place close in time, and that some of the four

Dhegiha groups who went up the Missouri River—the Osage, Omaha and Ponca, in addition to the Kansa—on occasion traveled together.

In any case, the Kansa moved up the south side of the Missouri River. Swanton states that during "at least a part of the eighteenth century they were on Missouri River above the mouth of the Kansas, but Lewis and Clark met them on the latter stream." Whether the American explorers encountered the main body of the Kansa or only a part of them is unknown. Hodge states that on their westward migration the Kansa made a brief halt at the mouth of the Kansas River, "after which they ascended the Missouri . . . until they reached the present N. boundary of Kansas, where they were attacked by the Cheyenne and compelled to retrace their steps." This conflict may have taken place about the middle of the eighteenth century. It has been definitely established that the Kansa lived at several places along the river named for them, ascending it at least as far as the Blue River.

The Kansa, as well as the other Dhegiha tribes, had patrilineal clans. According to Lowie these clans were generally divided into what may be termed subclans. The Kansa, he writes, "had seven larger units, which they called *those who sing together*; three comprised two clans, three were made up of three each."

The social structure of the Dhegiha tribes was extremely complicated, and a reliable analysis of it can be made only by a scientist thoroughly trained in this field. As an example, "kinship terms" may be cited. Lowie, a noted anthropologist, speaking in general of the Plains tribes, states that "nearly all of them call the father and the father's brother by a single word, while carefully separating the uncles on the father's from those on the mother's side. Correspondingly, they generally called a mother's sister 'mother,' but distinguished both the real mother and the maternal aunt from the paternal aunt. Since the natives were very logical in applying these terms, they also recognized a vast number of brothers and sisters; for persons who call the same individuals 'father' or 'mother' naturally regard one another as siblings."

Pointing out that "it appears the rule of descent has a good deal to do with the relationship system," Lowie explains that

> where the individual family and the local group are the only essential social divisions, people are as like to distinguish uncles from the father and aunts from the mother as we do. But where a one-side rule of descent prevails [such as the patrilineal of the Dhegiha], it tends to go with the classification described above.

That is, relatives are then considered with reference to whether they stem from the father's or the mother's side; accordingly, the maternal and paternal uncle cannot be called by the same name, but father and paternal uncle can be, because interest centers on the line of descent, not on physiological relations of individuals."

Among the patrilineal Siouans, a person could have many fathers and mothers. Lowie states that "in addition to the uncles on the father's side all his cousins would be reckoned as 'fathers' provided they were in the same clan as the father, and correspondingly for the mother's sisters and female cousins."

Although they adopted many cultural characteristics of true Plains tribes, the social structure of the Chiwere and Dhegiha groups remained similar, and in some instances identical, with Woodland peoples whose ancient homelands were east of the Mississippi. In Lowie's words, ". . . the resemblance cuts across linguistic family lines. Some Siouans are much nearer to certain Algonkians than to some other Siouans. The social structure and a kinship nomenclature in harmony with it has undoubtedly been diffused over a considerable number of tribes in the central states, irrespective of linguistic affinity. Whether the Algonkians or the Siouans were the originators, it is impossible to tell, for the features in question are not general in either stock."

The tribe that we know as the Kansa, or Kansas, called themselves the *Hutanga.* Swanton states that the name Kansa "derived from that of one of the major subdivisions; a shortened form Kaw is about equally current." Here again, like the Iowa and Missouri, prominently preserved is the name of a people who played a minor role in Indian history, who were relatively unaggressive and unenterprising.

Perhaps the most admirable qualities of the Kansa were two in number: (1) They held an unbounded and indestructible pride in themselves, and (2) they made uncommon efforts to instill high standards of morality in their young, and seemingly, to a greater extent than any other Plains people, they guarded the chastity of their women. They were conservative and intolerant. In the middle Plains they subsisted chiefly by hunting, and had only a casual interest in cultivating the soil. Their military operations were poorly executed, and even though many of them displayed courage on the battlefield, especially in defending themselves, they were frequently easily defeated by the Pawnee and other tribes.

The Kansa looked with equal contempt on the ways of other Indians and of white settlers. When the buffalo herds in their country were wiped out, they became desultory farmers only to avoid starvation. They considered it degrading to adopt any custom of the white man. When mission schools were built for them they refused to permit their children to be pupils.

A reservation was established for them in 1846 under a treaty by which they relinquished their claims to any other lands. The head-quarters of the reservation was at Council Grove, on the Neosho River, in Morris County. This tract was promptly invaded by white settlers, and the government made no effort to remove the illegal intruders. Still, the Kansa stubbornly clung to their earth lodges, tepees and corn patches for twenty-six years, most of the time eking out a miserable existence. Then, in 1873, the entire reservation, most of which already had been taken from them in brutal land grabs, was "sold" to white farmers. The money obtained, however, did not go to the Kansa. Much of it was stolen, but the Bureau of Indian Affairs claimed that the funds were used to purchase other lands for them in the Indian Territory.

Cheated of their rightful property and defenseless, the Kansa were ordered to move to Oklahoma. They went, but with no diminution of their prejudices and no loss of pride.

9   No more peaceful, industrious and progressive Indians ever lived in America than the PONCA. Yet the cruelties and injustices inflicted upon them by unconscionable politicians and government officials remain unsurpassed in western history.

When the Ohio River Valley was abandoned, the Ponca moved up the Mississippi and Missouri rivers. They apparently traveled with the Omaha, with whom, among the Dhegiha tribes, they were traditionally closely associated. Except for a few minor variations, the two groups spoke the same dialect of the Siouan tongue.

The Osage stayed in Missouri. The Kansa eventually settled on the Kansas River. The Ponca and Omaha, at some point on the Missouri River, turned inland and continued northward to the Pipestone Quarry in southwestern Minnesota. Evidently their relatives, the Dakota, did not welcome them in this region, and forced them to move westward.

Once more they reached the Missouri River. For an unknown reason, they separated at the mouth of White River, in the present state of South Dakota. It is said that the Ponca went on westward, perhaps ascending the White River, until they had come to the South Dakota badlands and the Black Hills. Probably stronger people forced them to turn back. They returned to the Missouri River once more, found the Omaha still approximately where they had left them and with them descended the river. The Ponca chose to settle on the Niobrara, and the Omaha established themselves a short distance to the south.

The way of life of the Ponca differed little from that of the other Dhegiha tribes who migrated westward to the eastern edge of the Great Plains. They dwelt in their Niobrara River villages during the period of the Oneota Culture, as did other Siouan groups who, in prehistoric times, left the middle-America woodlands and prairies. They were both farmers and hunters.

In their northern Nebraska homeland they were obviously in constant danger from surprise attack. Lowie describes one Ponca fort as harboring many earth lodges and having an embankment "over six feet in height. Situated on a bluff with a ravine at the rear, it could be entered from only one side and by passing for 200 yards along the ravine."

The meaning of *Ponca* is unknown, but it was the name by which the tribe identified itself. Marquette's autograph map of 1673 placed them on a stream believed to be the Missouri, near the Niobrara mouth, under the name *Pana*. Lewis and Clark found them in the same area in 1804. They were still there in 1856 when disaster struck.

An Indian agent reported that white settlers were beginning to intrude on lands awarded to the Ponca under a treaty made with them in 1825. In this pact the United States agreed to "receive the Poncar [sic] tribe of Indians into their friendship and under their protection, *and to extend to them from time to time such benefits and acts of kindness as may be convenient, and seem just and proper to the President of the United States.*" These words have been emphasized by the author, for, in reality, they relieved the government of all responsibility.

For more than thirty years, during which most other tribes of the upper Missouri country presented the United States with difficult problems and warred on traders, the military and on each other, the Ponca had been so peaceful that little notice had been taken of them in official records. An 1857 report to Washington said that white squatters were increasing in number on the Ponca Reservation, cutting trees, driving away game on which the Ponca depended, grazing herds in Ponca cornfields, building farms and stealing Ponca livestock.

The protection which the United States had promised failed to materialize. President James Buchanan obviously found it *inconvenient* to extend any benefits or perform any *acts of kindness*. It was *convenient*, however for the government to force the Ponca to sign a new treaty "for the purpose of extinguishing their title to all the lands occupied and claimed by them, except small portions on which to colonize and domesticate them." The Indian Bureau announced that "this proceeding was deemed necessary in order to obtain such control over these Indians *as to prevent their interference with our settlements*, which are rapidly extending in that direction."

The Senate didn't find it *convenient* to ratify the treaty until 1859. Meanwhile, the Ponca, believing it to be in effect, proceeded in good faith to carry out their end of the bargain. They complied with the provisions by abandoning their settlements, and moving to the "small portions" which they presumed would be their permanent homeland. As a result, said an Indian agent, they were quickly "reduced to a state of desperation and destitution."

A detailed account of the sufferings of the Ponca is not within the scope of this work. It should be recorded, however, that under the Treaty of 1858, the government agreed to "protect the Ponca in the possession of this tract of land, and their property and persons thereon . . . to pay them annuities annually for thirty years—$12,000 for the first five years, then $10,000 for ten years, then $8,000 for fifteen years; to expend $20,000 for their subsistence during the first year, for building houses, etc., to establish schools and to build mills, mechanics shops, etc. . . ."

These agreements were never fulfilled. After five years of waiting for sufficient funds to enable the Ponca to progress, an agent wrote that the agency building was "constantly surrounded by a hungry crowd begging for food. I am warned by the military to keep the Poncas within the limits of the reservation, but this is an impossibility. There is nothing within its limits. . . . The Poncas have behaved well—quite as well, if not better than, under like circumstances, the same number of whites would have done."

Some humane persons in Washington managed to persuade the Congress to make small appropriations from time to time to keep all the Ponca from starving to death. The amount of the funds was begrudgingly increased, but not until the plight and treatment of the Ponca had begun to attract national attention. The good use to which the Ponca put the money that was made available to them and their indefatigable efforts to improve their property comprised incontestable evidence of their sincere desire to become a progressive, peaceful and permanent segment of American society. Good houses were built, lands were cultivated, a mission church was constructed, and when, after waiting eight years, a school finally was built for them, they willingly sent their children to it. Not only white settlers but wild bands of Dakota Sioux stole their horses and cattle. Drought and locusts destroyed their crops. Floods ruined their farms. But they refused to accept defeat and after each loss set out to rebuild with undiminished vigor.

For nearly two decades they courageously bore all the burdens of evil thrust upon them. Then, in 1876, they suffered a blow from which they were unable to recover.

White "voters" demanded that the Ponca Reservation be taken from them and opened to settlement, and Washington officials decided that the tribe should be moved to the Indian Territory (Oklahoma). It was not necessary to have a treaty under which this political scheme could be executed, for Indian tribes were no longer considered foreign nations. All that was needed was for the government to obtain the Ponca's "consent," after which they could be removed.

How that consent was obtained was related in one of the most moving documents to be found in the history of the Indians. The author was a Ponca leader, Standing Bear, and his statement appeared in the 1876 annual report of the Bureau of Indian Affairs.

The Ponca were moved at bayonet point to the Indian Territory, and left stranded on a plain without money, food or equipment. Standing Bear and several other leaders ran away and returned north in another desperate effort to save the tribe's Nebraska lands. They were arrested by soldiers and thrown into jail.

The incredibly cruel treatment of the Ponca, the destruction of their homes, farms and all their possessions, aroused indignation throughout the Midwest and the East. Newspapers condemned the government's actions. Many individuals and organizations contributed money to finance a court suit to have them returned to their former homes and to be recompensed for their real losses.

The Ponca who had run away from the Indian Territory were released from custody by a federal judge in Omaha in a celebrated decision. Attorneys for the government contended that an Indian was not "entitled to protection of the writ of habeas corpus, not being a person or citizen under the law." The court ruled against them.

So great became the national clamor for justice in the Ponca case that a Presidential commission was appointed to make an investigation. It was determined that without question the Ponca owned their Nebraska lands in fee simple, and the titles were without a cloud. Yet, the government had driven them away as if they had been squatters without a legal claim of any kind to the property.

The commission was able to effect an agreement which reportedly was satisfactory to the Ponca. Under it, the greater portion of the tribe remained in Oklahoma, and the others returned to their farms along the Niobrara.

But greedy white Americans, repudiating all laws of justice, all concepts of morality, and abetted by unconscionable politicians, were the victors. They had succeeded in breaking and dividing a small peaceful people whose loyalty to the United States had never wavered.

10　The OMAHA were spared a fate similar to that of the Ponca by the unrelenting efforts of a woman, Alice C. Fletcher, a distinguished ethnologist of Washington, D.C.

One of the Dhegiha tribes that migrated westward from the Ohio Valley region, the Omaha retained many characteristics of the Woodland Culture that was their way of life east of the Mississippi River. In the words of Lowie, these Siouan groups "have the same form of patrilineal clan organization as the Central Algonkians and the Winnebago, and with it went the same mode of classifying relatives.* In vital aspects of social life, the Omaha resemble the Algonkian Menomini of the Woodlands more than they do their fellow Siouans." For example, the Omaha made wooden bowls from black walnut burrs, mortars from round pieces of tree trunks, other wooden utensils, such as spoons and ladles that could be hooked over a bowl's rim, and a large assortment of utilitarian pottery vessels, a craft uncommon among less sedentary Plains people who lived principally by hunting, for heavy earthenware was breakable and difficult to transport. Tattooing was practiced, although not as highly developed by the Omaha or other Dhegiha groups as it was among some Woodland tribes, especially those south of Kentucky. Nevertheless, tattooed designs were not merely decorative but were often socially significant. Lowie notes that an eminent Omaha, for instance, "could get prestige for himself and a daughter recently come of age by having her tattooed in the center of the forehead with a black circle representing the sun and with a four-pointed star on her chest to symbolize the night."

Yet a true Plains culture soon influenced the Omaha after their westward migration. They dwelt in the cold months in villages of earth lodges, but in the summer, after crops were planted, they set out to hunt buffalo and other big game on

*See Part Four, Chap. 8.

the Plains, and lived in portable skin lodges. These tepees were erected in a circle, and each clan was assigned to a definite area.

The meaning of the name *Omaha* has been unquestionably established. Appropriately it signifies "those going against the current," for when they put their ancient Ohio and Indiana homes behind them for the last time and descended the Ohio River, they turned northward and westward, first up the Mississippi, and then up the Missouri. Whether *Omaha*—sometimes shortened to *Maha*—was always their own name is doubtful, but no other has come to light. It became their name, however, when they undertook their westward migration, and by it they became known to history.

The Omaha had a rather rigid political structure, though in no sense autocratic. At the head of their government were two chiefs, but they seldom, if ever, made final decisions in any important matter without consulting with a tribal council, usually consisting of seven titular leaders. Quarrels were settled by intermediaries, rarely by force. In some cases sacred pipes were placed between combatants, and they served as a warning, if not a command, to them to desist. When corporal punishment was decreed for a lawbreaker, it was inflicted by police appointed by the council. Leaders were chosen for each buffalo hunt, and their orders were rigidly enforced, for the welfare of all the people was at stake. A disobedient individual might be lashed by the police. The council took action in murder cases. The customary penalty was banishment for four years. During this period, according to Fletcher and LaFlesche,

> the murderer was obliged to remain on the edge of the camp and hold no intercourse with anyone but his immediate family, who might seek him out and furnish him with provisions. The duration of the penalty was in a measure dependent on the sentiments of the mourning kin, for as soon as they relented the exile was allowed to return. That is to say, homicide despite tribal interference ranked after all as a tort: it was not the tribe that exacted punishment but the suffering family, and the council intervened not to exact a condign penalty but to satisfy the private feeling of revenge and prevent civil dissension with consequent weakening of the community.

When they separated from the Ponca at the confluence of the Missouri and Niobrara rivers, the Omaha moved a short distance farther south and settled on Bow Creek in what is now eastern

Nebraska. This separation took place in prehistoric times but, as Swanton states, the Omaha "continued from that time forward in the same general region, the west side of the Missouri River between the Platte and the Niobrara."

In 1854 the Omaha were "induced" to sign a scandalous treaty under which they "sold" all their lands, except a small reserve in Dakota County, Nebraska, to which they were forced to move in 1855. White settlers took over their former country. In 1865 the government took a part of their reservation from them for the Winnebago.

For more than a decade they clung precariously to their homes and farms, with white farmers, supported by their congressional and local politicians, demanding continuously that the Omaha be sent to Indian Territory.

Then the noted ethnologist, Alice C. Fletcher, went on the "warpath" on Capitol Hill. Her humanitarian efforts generated sufficient pressure to persuade Congress to grant the Omaha lands in severalty, with a promise that they would be granted citizenship. Miss Fletcher was given the authority to allot the lands. Washington officials were happy to be rid of both her and the problem.

11   In *A Tour of the Prairies*, published in 1835, Washington Irving wrote:

> Near by were a group of Osages; stately fellows; stern and simple in garb and aspect. They wore no ornaments; their dress consisted merely of blankets, leggings and moccasins. Their heads were bare; their hair was cropped close, except a bristling ridge on top, like the crest of a helmet, with a long scalp look hanging behind. They had fine Roman countenances, and broad deep chests; and, as they generally wore their blankets wrapped around their loins, so as to leave the bust and arms bare, they looked like so many bronze figures. The Osages are the finest looking Indians I have ever seen in the West.

This description of the OSAGE appeared in print nearly three decades after the United States had begun to take from them their Missouri and Arkansas homeland, and about the same number of decades before they were driven to their final place of confinement in the Indian Territory.

The Osage were the most important and the largest tribe of the Dhegiha division of the Siouan linguistic family. When they dwelt in Ohio they were greater numerically than when they migrated westward, for they included the Quapaw, who separated from them to go down the Mississippi. The Osage pushed up the Mississippi and up the Missouri, stopping finally when they reached the river that bears their name. In this region they remained for centuries, until the pressures of American settlement drove them out of it.

The author and Indian scholar, John Joseph Mathews, himself an Osage, writes that his people called themselves *Ni-U-Ko'n-Ska*, signifying "Children of the Middle Waters." A number of ethnologists and linguists assert that their own name was *Wazhazhe*, and the best that early French traders could do with this word as they heard it was *Osage*. In any case, the corruption has survived, applied to all of them, but

Swanton thinks that *Wazhazhe* "is probably an extension of the name of one of the three bands of which the tribe is composed."

The Osage were good farmers, planting an estimated one-third of an acre for every man, woman and child of the tribe. They were excellent hunters. Their own land was rich in game, but they also went on annual hunts to the Great Plains to kill hundreds of buffalo, which supplied the largest number and the most valuable products of any animal. They were courageous and ferocious warriors, and were often in conflict with several tribes at the same time. This was especially true in the eighteenth century, when they were at war with most of the tribes of the Plains, as well as some people of the Midwestern Woodlands, and to many their name was a synonym for *enemy*.

Until the beginning of the nineteenth century, according to contemporary historians, the Osage were divided into two principal groups, the Big Osage, by far the largest, and the Little Osage. About 1802, a chieftain called Big Track led about half of the Big Osage southwestward to the Arkansas River, in this way creating a third division popularly known as the Arkansas Band. This situation prevailed at the beginning of the American period, following the Louisiana Purchase. Scientific investigations, however, have shown that apparently three divisions also existed far back in prehistoric times.

The noted ethnologist and linguist, J. O. Dorsey, who made a thorough study of Osage traditions, stated that they recognized three closely amalgamated branches, which at one time may have been independent tribes. At first, Dorsey relates, they were separated into two tribes, the Tsishu, or peace people, who kept to the left and lived on vegetal foods, and the Wazhazhe, or war people, who kept to the right and lived on the meat of wild animals. In time these two tribes began to exchange commodities, and eventually the Tsishu came into possession of corn and pumpkins. The united groups later encountered the Hangka, a warlike people who also lived on animals, and eventually were able to make peace with them. The Hangka joined the tribe on the war side.

This amalgamation created a political imbalance, as each group was composed of seven gentes, giving the war side fourteen and the peace side only seven. A reorganization was effected, and each side contained an equal number of gentes, seven in number, but the three divisions continued to exist. Swanton writes that the functions of the various gentes were differentiated to a certain extent, problems of war being undertaken by the war gentes and peace making by the peace gentes, and the "Tsishu gentes are also said to have had the care and naming of children. Heralds were chosen from certain special gentes, and certain others monopolized the manufacture of moccasins, war standards, and war pipes." Having migrated from the Ohio Valley, established themselves in the prairie-woodland environment of Missouri and hunted on the Great Plains, the culture of the Osages contained characteristics of both Woodland and Plains cultures. In Missouri they evolved into a marginal prairie-woodland people. Wedel suggests that in time they "acquired a strong Plains bias, adopted many of the typical artifacts and practices of their westerly neighbors, and finally assumed an active role in the equestrian bison-hunting life of the semi-horticultural peoples to whom they were geographically marginal."

The mythology of the Osage equals, if not surpasses, in beauty and imagination that of any other Indian people. Their creation myth relates that they came from the stars, originating in the lowest of four upper worlds and ascending to the highest, where they were given souls. Then they descended until they came to a red oak tree, which supported the lowest of the upper worlds, and by climbing down through its branches they reached the earth. Neither the earth nor anything upon it had a name, and they gave names to all the earth's features, and to all the animals and trees and grasses and birds, as well as to the sky, the sun, the moon and the stars.

"The Children of the Middle Waters," Mathews writes,

> had begun to reason long before they came to build fantasies upon the foundations of their biological instincts and upon their mysterious urges. They had begun long before to fumble toward the Light which their mental development would demand that they recognize. They felt more now than the urges of food-getting and mating; there was the third urge that came with thought. This was Wah'Kon, the Mystery Force, and in their urgency to come to some understanding of this life-force, they knew great fear and confusion, and they could only build their own framework into which they would try to fit this Wah'Kon and therefore bring it within the boundaries of their conceptions. They had been busy for perhaps centuries building a ritualistic cage for this Wah'Kon, the Mystery Force, that they might have it under control, materialize it out of the world of abstractions, so that they might know relief or protection from their own fears and uncertainties.

Long before the first European found them, they had not only given names to everything on the earth and in the sky, but they "also knew how they got there and why they were there, and they also had fumbled toward an understanding of the Wah'Kon and had a very comforting interpretation under which they dwelt."

In their humility the Children of the Middle Waters spoke of themselves as the Little Ones. Before they departed from the Sky Lodge, Grandfather the Sun taught them to make arrows as straight as his rays, and he made for them a bow from the Osage orange tree, and another from the antler of the wapiti. Earth animals taught them about foods and gave them furs.

Wak'Kon-Tah, the Great Force who maintained order in the sky, Mathews relates, "struck the long grass of the late summer or early spring with his crooked firelance and the flames raced, and the Little Ones learned about fire. At night they would sit about their own captured fire and look up at their brothers who had remained in the sky, gradually becoming aware of the seasonal changes and the various positions of the Big Dipper, as he wheeled about the North Star. They called the Morning Star the Male Star and the Evening Star the Female Star."

It took the Americans only the number of years that could be counted on the fingers of one hand to take the homeland of the Osage away from them. In November, 1808, five years after the Louisiana Purchase, Osage leaders were ordered to meet with federal government emissaries, near a place on the Missouri River which the Indians called Fire Prairie, to "make a treaty." Representing the United States were Governor Meriwether Lewis of Missouri, his old exploring companion, Clark, and the fur trader and Indian agent Pierre Chouteau.

Following a council, Chouteau told the Osage representatives: "You have heard this treaty explained to you. Those who now come forward and sign it shall be considered the friends of the United States and treated accordingly. Those who refuse to come forward and sign it shall be considered enemies of the United States and treated accordingly."

In substance, the Osage replied that as the United States was strong and powerful and they were poor and weak, they had no choice but to "touch the feather"—that is, to put their marks on the paper.

The purpose of the treaty was twofold: (1) To advance the Jeffersonian policy of pushing all Indians into the unsettled West, and (2) to obtain for white settlement the extremely rich lands occupied by the Osage, who were looked upon as troublesome Indians.

Under the treaty, the Osage were forced to cede to the United States virtually all their territorial claims in the modern states of Missouri and Arkansas. The little land left to them was acquired by the United States through subsequent treaties. The Osage were forced onto the southwestern Plains. Not until 1870 did Congress get around to establishing the boundaries of a reservation for them in Indian Territory.

12   It is improbable that the combined population of the seven
Siouan Chiwere and Dhegiha tribes considered in this part
exceeded twenty thousand men, women and children at the
beginning of the historical period.

However, the memory of these tribes has been preserved
in numerous place names:

TRIBE	PLACE NAME
Kansa and Kaw	Kansas City, Missouri. The state of Kansas, and in it the Kansas River and Kansas City. Towns in Illinois, Alabama, Ohio, Oklahoma and Wisconsin.
Ponca	Ponca River in South Dakota. Ponca City in Oklahoma, and towns in Arkansas and Nebraska.
Omaha	The city of Omaha, Nebraska, and towns in Arkansas, Georgia, Illinois, Texas, Kentucky and Virginia.
Osage	The Osage River in Kansas and Missouri. A tributary of the Gasconade River in Missouri. A creek in Arkansas, and towns in Arkansas, Illinois, Iowa, Oklahoma, Minnesota, Texas, West Virginia, Missouri, Wyoming and Kansas.
Iowa	The state of Iowa, and in it Iowa City, two rivers, a falls and several small places. A community in Texas, a hill in California.
Missouri	The state of Missouri. The Missouri River, and places in Missouri, Texas and Iowa.
Oto and Otoe	Towns in Iowa and Missouri, and a county and village in Nebraska.

PART FIVE

The Sioux of the Northern Woodlands and the Northern Great Plains

1 Two kinds of warfare ravaged the Great Lakes region in the first half of the seventeenth century. The primary causes generating them could be distinguished, but they were not altogether without a relationship. There was the intertribal warfare, born of traditional enmities and the irrepressible urge to plunder, and there was the warfare that started when the French brought their metal utensils and tools and their guns into the realm of people still living in the Stone Age.

A frenzied demand for these miraculous products was created, and with it came vicious struggles, not only to acquire them, but to control distribution of them—economic warfare. The French wanted furs, and Indians could supply them in great quantity, but intertribal conflicts disrupted trade, and often to the extent that development which would have been possible under other conditions was prevented. Therefore, the French fur traders of Quebec and Montreal, notably the famed Samuel de Champlain, wanted peace among the warring tribes in the undeveloped West, and at last, in 1634, they sent the great explorer, Jean Nicolet, who had lived for a number of years among the Indians and spoke several native languages, to attempt to halt the fighting.

Nicolet also was given another mission. For years vague reports had filtered into Quebec about a strong, vicious, warlike people who practiced cannibalism. They were called WINNEBAGO, but sometimes Indians spoke of them as the People of the Sea, for there was a tale that at one time they had dwelt on a great body of water that lay only a short distance to the west of their present home, and that they still traded with other peoples of this western sea.

Champlain never ceased to believe that a water passage from Georgian Bay to the Pacific existed, and the reference to the western sea prompted him, as well as other Quebec traders, to assume that it was near the Orient. So confident

were they that the people of the western sea who traded with the
Winnebago were Chinese—some traders held the theory they were
Tartars—that Nicolet was provided with a costume that would mark
him as a man of high rank and cause him to be treated with respect.

Nicolet passed through the Straits of Mackinac and discovered Lake
Michigan. He had with him, according to the Jesuit Relations of 1643,
some 400 Algonquians. The flotilla of large fur-trade canoes passed
down the west shore of Lake Michigan and up Green Bay, a region
never before entered by a white man. Nicolet kept handy his oriental
costume, a magnificent mandarin robe of crimson brocade decorated
with brilliantly colored flowers and birds. From Green Bay he ascended Fox River. When scouts informed him he was nearing a large
settlement, he donned the robe. Wearing it, he strode into the town in
regal fashion, carrying a pistol in each hand. Hyde suggests that he
must have fired the pistols, for the women and children fled in terror,
"and called him a spirit who held thunder in both hands."

Nicolet was the first Frenchman, indeed the first European, to reach
a Siouan people in the north. Winnebago leaders welcomed him with
great respect, and gave a feast in his honor, but they knew nothing
about a western sea, nothing about Tartars, nothing about a place
called China.

Determinedly Nicolet went on. From Lake Winnebago he ascended
Fox River. When at last he decided to turn back, the Winnebago told
him that he was only three days' travel by a portage and water from a
great river that emptied into a sea far to the south. He had heard of the
Mississippi, and he returned believing that a waterway reached
Spanish Mexico. As far as he was concerned, that was important
geographical information but of little value to him, for he was looking
for a way to the Orient, and he wanted nothing to do with the Spanish.

The Winnebago had been in their Wisconsin homeland a very long
time before Nicolet found them, but how long is a question archaeology
has not yet answered. They were an important tribe of the Chiwere
division of the Siouan linguistic family, perhaps a "main root" from
which other tribes of the group sprang. They spoke a dialect that was
very similar to that of the Tutelo of Virginia and North Carolina, but
there is no archaeological proof that they were ever in the Ohio Valley
region, from which the Tutelo are believed to have migrated to the
Southeast. They called themselves *Hotcangara*, signifying "people of
the real (or big) speech," which may or may not indicate predominance
linguistically in the Chiwere branch.

How or why they acquired the uncomplimentary name of Winnebago are puzzles scientists have not been able to explain. Any number of theories have been advanced, none of them supported by a shred of irrefutable evidence. *Winnebago* comes from the Algonquian tongue spoken by the Fox and Sauk Indians, and in what is probably the most literal translation it means "people of the filthy water." Certainly it could not have been applied to the beautiful, clean, clear waters of Lake Michigan, Green Bay and the streams of Wisconsin as they were in prehistoric times.

Yet, they were known to other tribes as Winnebago when the French traders of the St. Lawrence first heard of them, and obviously, therefore, before that time. Had it come down through legend or tradition that in some ancient period they actually had dwelt beside a sea in which salt made the water unusable, therefore *filthy*? It is difficult to imagine anything more improbable. Champlain incorrectly placed the Winnebago in Michigan on one of his maps, drawn before Nicolet visited them, and called them *La Nation des Puants.* A French missionary wrote in 1636 that the Iroquois name for the Winnebago also meant "stinkards." In the Jesuit Relations of 1638 they are referred to as *des gentes puants*, or "stinking people." Thwaites bluntly states the belief that it was the Winnebago and not the water that stank.

Early French documents repeatedly speak of the Winnebago as sodomites and cannibals. Archaeological discoveries verify that they consumed human flesh. Their cannibalistic practices during their close association with the people of Aztalan have been mentioned in previous chapters, and need not be recounted here. It should be noted, however, that long before they were driven westward from Wisconsin by the pressures of civilization they had abandoned the custom of roasting and devouring captured enemies.

All Indian peoples pay obeisance to supernaturals; all seek to gain favor from spirits and to ward off evil influences through some form of ritual. Some believe in a supreme being, others do not. The religion of the Winnebago, however, not only dealt with deity worship and ameliorating the practical difficulties encountered on their earthly road. They believed that when death came they would go to live forever in an afterworld, and they sought through both individual and communal prayer to prepare themselves for life in this mysterious realm.

Because from time immemorial they were Woodland Indians, the religious doctrine of the Winnebago included beliefs identical with those of some other peoples of a similar environment with whom they were in contact, even peoples who at times were deadly enemies. Dorsey states* that a Winnebago figure known as Earthmaker "corresponds to the *Gitchi Manitou* of the Central Algonquian tribes. The mythology consists of large cycles relating to the five personages whom Earthmaker sent out to free the world from giants and evil spirits." He adds that although "there are evidences of Central Algonquian influence, the Winnebago mythology shows a much more intimate relation with that of other Siouan tribes." Underwood writes that four of the five deputies of Earthmaker, or Creator, failed in their missions, and Earthmaker then created Hare, and "Hare went down to earth and, to have a real kinship with human beings, he entered the womb of a virgin. Even there he heard the people weeping and shrieking, so he burst out prematurely, killing his mother. He destroyed the evil ones and thrust them down under the earth, and his grandmother (earth or fertility) produced corn and tobacco from her body. But the people . . . still mourned because their life was short. So he gave them the final gift put in his power by the Creator, the gift of reincarnation."

Regarding the social organization of the Winnebago, Radin states that it "is based on two phratries known as the Upper or Air, and the Lower or Earth divisions. The Upper division contains four clans, Thunderbird, War People, Eagle and Pigeon,* and the Lower division eight clans, the Bear, Wolf, Water-spirit, Deer-Elk, Buffalo, Fish and Snake. An Upper individual must marry a Lower individual, and vice versa. . . . The Thunderbird and Bear clans are regarded as the leading clans of their respective phratries."

Both of these clans had definite functions. The Thunderbird Clan was the "peace lodge," over which the chief of the tribe presided. It served as a kind of tribunal in which disputes were adjudicated. The Bear Clan was a "war or disciplinary lodge," holding the power to kill prisoners or punish lawbreakers, and it was in charge of the camping circle during a tribal hunt. Although it is believed that all clans participated in building effigy mounds—there are many Siouan mounds of this type in southern Wisconsin—a member of one clan could not be buried by members of another clan of the same phratry.

On several occasions the Winnebago suffered calamitous reverses in

*In Hodge (q.v.).
*Extinct in the nineteenth century.

warfare. They were daring and vicious aggressors, and the victories they achieved resulted in retaliatory attacks by strong forces. The earliest French traders and missionaries recorded accounts relating how in late prehistoric times, they disastrously defeated the Illini. Other Algonquian tribes then rallied to the support of the Illini, and almost destroyed the Winnebago. These tales may or may not be true. There seems to be little doubt, however, that the Winnebago wantonly murdered and ate a group of Ottawa who possessed French goods and were attempting to extend their trade into the Wisconsin area. According to La Pothérie, the Ottawa called upon their allies to assist them in an offensive against the Winnebago. It was carried out the following summer. Overwhelmed, the Winnebago fled in confusion. Some of the Chiwere groups reportedly scattered into the west, refusing to become embroiled in the fighting, but their identities are unknown. They may have been the Iowa, Oto, Missouri and Hidatsa. The Winnebago attempted to escape to the south, but were pursued and suffered heavy losses. La Pothérie states that pestilence broke out among them at this time and claimed many lives. Nicolet estimated that the Winnebago had four thousand warriors. If La Pothérie is correct, only about fifteen hundred survived the assault by the Ottawa and their allies.

The French became firmly established in the western Great Lakes region. Trading posts and missions were built. The Winnebago and the Algonquian Menominee became closely associated, and both tribes opened their lands to the Potawatomi and the Ottawa who were driven westward by the Iroquois, and gave shelter as well to the Sauk and Fox when they were driven from southern Michigan.

The Winnebago had rapidly recovered from their battlefield disasters and were again a strong tribe. Although they remained proud and haughty, their belligerency had been supplanted by a peaceful attitude, and for many years they maintained amicable relationships with the tribes surrounding them. After the fall of the French power in Canada in 1760 they were slow to transfer their allegiance to Great Britain, but when they did they remained firm in their new fealty. They sided with the British in the American Revolution. Winnebago warriors fought beside British soldiers in several battles of the War of 1812.

The inevitable occurred—Americans wanted their lands. Under coercive legal and political powers they signed a treaty in 1825 ceding all their territorial claims in Wisconsin. They were given in return a comparatively small reservation on the west side of the Mississippi above the upper Iowa River. There many of them died of smallpox. In 1846 soldiers were sent to drive them, by force of arms, if necessary, to a reservation in Minnesota, north of the Minnesota River. Force of arms was necessary, as many refused to leave Iowa willingly. They had been concentrated in the reservation north of the Minnesota River only two years, when soldiers again came and drove them to another location. Twice more, in 1853 and 1856, they were forced to move. In the latter year a new treaty gave them "in perpetuity" a reservation at Blue Earth, Minnesota.

Believing, or at least praying, that they would be allowed to remain in their Blue Earth home, they demonstrated their desire to become self-supporting peaceful residents. In 1860, the Commissioner of Indian Affairs reported that their progress "in agricultural growths is particularly marked with success. . . . The agent's efforts have been directed to giving to each Indian his own allotment of land. . . . Wigwams are becoming as scarce as houses were two years ago. . . . The school is in a flourishing condition."

In 1862, after years of waiting for the federal government to keep its promises, the Santee Sioux of Minnesota went on the warpath. The Winnebago refused to join their relatives in the uprising. "While it may be true that a few of the Winnebagos were engaged in the atrocities of the [Santee] Sioux, the tribe, as such is no more justly responsible for their acts than our Government would be for a pirate who happened to have been born in our territory," said the 1862 annual report of the Interior Department. "Notwithstanding this, the exasperation of the people of Minnesota appears to be nearly as great toward the Winnebagos as toward the Sioux. They demand that the Winnebagos shall be removed from the limits of the State. The Winnebagos are unwilling to move. Yet the people of Minnesota are so excited that not a Winnebago can leave his reservation without risk of being shot; and as they have never received their promised implements of agriculture, and the game on their reservation is exhausted, and their arms have been taken from them, *they are starving.*"

Politicians, land companies and merchants added their cries to the clamor. The Congress tore up its treaty with the Winnebago and ordered that they be relocated "on the Missouri River somewhere within a hundred miles of Fort Randall, where it is not doubted they will be secure from any danger of intrusion from whites . . ." The people of Minnesota swarmed over the Winnebago lands, snarling and fighting among themselves for possession of them.

"The cruelty of the forced removal by troops," this author previously wrote,* "was augmented by the inconceivably absurd manner in which it was carried out. The Winnebago, numbering only a mere two thousand now, were taken from Mankato down the St. Peters to Fort Snelling, loaded on steamboats, thence down the Mississippi to the Missouri, and up the Missouri to the new reservation (called Crow Creek) assigned to them. The reservation was 1,363 miles from the Missouri mouth, but only about 300 miles by land from their old Minnesota dwelling place. Men, women and children jammed like animals on the boats were transported more than 2,000 miles, when they might have reached their destination easily and without great hardship by wagon caravans on an overland journey of only 300 miles.

"The Government required the Winnebago to pay the cost of the removal from treaty funds long due them."

A contemporary report cited by Manypenny stated that they "were very much crowded . . . without attention or medical supplies. All the Indians were excluded from the cabin of the boat, and confined to the lower and upper decks. It was in May and to go among them on the lower deck was suffocating. They were fed on hard bread and mess pork, much of it not cooked. Confinement in such a mass and want of proper food created much sickness, such as diarrhea and fevers. For weeks they died at the rate of three to four per day."

The Winnebago had been promised good homes and good lands, but were unceremoniously herded from the boats onto a sandy beach. Around them as far as they could see was nothing but a barren plain burning in the summer heat. Not a house had been built. They had been promised farm implements. None came. They had been promised food. Very little came in the summer, and much of it was rotten.

The thieves in the Indian Bureau and the suppliers to whom they awarded contracts were having a field day. Soldiers patrolled the area to keep the starving, sick Winnebago from leaving to hunt or to attempt to get food from other tribes. Some escaped and fled to the Omaha in Nebraska, where they were welcomed and protected, but others were shot down while attempting to leave. Squaws were raped by drunken troopers.

Some oxen which had been used to pull freight wagons across the plains were killed in January, and the carcasses piled in the snow. This meat was to feed the Winnebago until the following June. Wrote Manypenny: ". . . it was black and very poor—the greater part only

*Terrell (1972).

skin and bone. . . . There was thrown into a vat beef, beef heads, entrails of the beeves, some beans, flour and pork. This mass was then cooked by steam. . . . When that was done, all the Indians were ordered to come with their pails and get it. . . . It was about the consistency of very thin gruel. . . . It had a very offensive odor. It had the odor of the entrails of the beeves . . . the settlings in the vat smelled like carrion, like decomposed meat. . ."

Despite the danger involved, so many Winnebago managed to slip away and take refuge with the Omaha that at last the government concluded that they might as well all go. So land was taken away from the Omaha for them.

"The case of the Winnebagos," said the 1863 report of the Commissioner of Indian Affairs, "is one of peculiar hardship. . . . It is to be feared that it will be many years before their confidence in the good faith of our Government, in its professed desire to ameliorate and improve their condition, will be restored."

He was right. As these words are written, it's been a hundred and ten years.

2 The first known homelands in historical times of the Siouan tribes considered in this part were:

WINNEBAGO: Eastern Wisconsin.

HIDATSA: On Missouri River near mouth of Heart River, North Dakota.

MANDAN: Same area as the Hidatsa.

MDEWKANTON: Eastern Minnesota.

WAHPETON: North-central Minnesota.

WAHPEKUTE: North-central Minnesota.

SISSETON: Central Minnesota.

YANKTON: Northern Minnesota.

YANKTONAI: Northern Minnesota.

HUNKPATINA: Northern Minnesota.

BRULÉ: Central South Dakota.

HUNKPAPA: In North Dakota west of Missouri River.

MINICONJOU: North-central South Dakota.

OGLALA: North-central South Dakota.

OOHENONPA: Northwestern South Dakota.

SANS ARCS: In the area of the Hunkpapa.

SIHASAPA: In the same area as the Sans Arcs.

ASSINIBOIN: In the vicinity of the Lake of the Woods.

CROW: First encountered as a separate tribe on the Yellowstone River in Montana, but previously were a part of the Hidatsa.

3 On the upper Missouri River, for centuries before the beginning of the historical period in this region, stood the walled towns of the MANDAN and the HIDATSA, the northernmost tribes of the Chiwere division of the Siouan linguistic family.

It is generally believed by scientists that the Mandan were the first Siouan people to establish themselves in this part of the North Dakota area. Archaeological discoveries indicate that they reached the upper Missouri in the vicinity of the mouth of White River, but they may have lived farther downstream for a time at an earlier period, and they may have dwelt for some years in the course of their westward migration on the Mississippi. In one respect, however, language provides convincing evidence of their movements that predates recovered material objects denoting their presence in the Missouri River Valley.

The closest connections of the Mandan tongue, or dialect, are with the Siouan Tutelo of the Southeast and the Winnebago. This fact gives rise to several questions, but one postulation seems wholly justified. It is that at some remote period both the Mandan and the Tutelo dwelt in the Ohio River Valley region. The Tutelo migrated to the southeastern Piedmont, and the Mandan went northward.

The time of the Mandan migration is unknown. It may have taken place during the period of the Hopewell, or Mound Builder, Culture. This culture spread northward from the Ohio Valley through Illinois into Wisconsin and across the Mississippi. When it faded in this area, according to Hyde, "a Hopewell offshoot, the Effigy Mound Culture of Wisconsin, continued to grow. It spread westward to the mouth of the Wisconsin River and then across the Mississippi. . . . This Effigy Mound Culture was undoubtedly Siouan in origin. It had its beginning in a Siouan area in Wisconsin." In this area were the Winnebago, Iowa, Oto and Missouri tribes, and Hyde adds that "we must suppose that the Mandans and the Hidatsa-Crow tribe, all closely connected linguistically with the Winnebagoes, were in Wisconsin or northern Illinois and took part in the making of Effigy Mound Culture."

Although they were long neighbors of the Mandan on the upper Missouri, the Hidatsa apparently wandered first farther to the north and west from their Midwestern homeland. At this time, and until well into the historical period, the Hidatsa and the people who would come to be known as the Crow were a single tribe. What is known of the quarrel that resulted in a permanent separation will be recounted in the chapter on the Crow. The Hidatsa hunted as far west as eastern Montana, and perhaps northward into Saskatchewan. When the first white traders met them the Mandan had distinct traditions of an eastern origin, but the Hidatsa traditions went no farther back than a homeland in eastern North Dakota, believed to be in the vicinity of Devil's Lake.

It was probably not until relatively late in the prehistoric period that the Hidatsa became permanently settled on the upper Missouri. Ruins of their early villages have been found about the confluence of the Missouri and Knife rivers. Previously they had lived entirely by hunting and the gathering of wild plant foods, but when they settled at Knife River they associated themselves with the semisedentary Mandan, whose towns were only a short distance downstream, and from them they learned to farm.*

The Mandan were among the most competent and successful agriculturists of the northern Great Plains. From the time of their discovery by French *voyageurs* until well into the American period reports relate how nomadic tribes journeyed annually to trade for maize at their villages. It is said that the Mandan grew more corn than any other Upper Missouri tribe, in good years harvesting as much as twenty or twenty-five bushels per acre from several thousand acres.†

The meaning of the word *mandan* is uncertain, but Swanton states that it is probably a corruption of the name *Mawatani*, which was applied to them by the Dakota Sioux. In early historical times they called themselves *Numakaki*, signifying "men" or "people."

*The villages of the Arikara, who had once been a part of the Skidi Pawnee, were farther down the Missouri in South Dakota. They were a powerful and troublesome people. Although the course of events eventually would bring them into close relationship with the Mandan and Hidatsa, they belonged to the Caddoan linguistic family, and, therefore, their history is beyond the scope of this book.
†The Arikara also grew large amounts, and the Hidatsa, adopting the methods of the Mandan, became highly successful agriculturists.

When the Hidatsa became their neighbors the Mandan called them *Minitari*, meaning "they crossed the water," in this case the Missouri River. How the Hidatsa identified themselves previously is not known. Hidatsa is said on doubtful authority to mean "willows." The ethnologist, Washington Matthews, who studied the tribe, stated that Hidatsa was merely the name of one of their early towns. The Crow, who separated from them, called them *A-me-she*, a most appropriate name, for it means "people who live in earth houses." Missouri River traders interpreted the sign language in a manner that resulted in their being dubbed *Gros Ventres*, or "Big Bellies." The same name was applied by the traders to the Atsina, a detached band of the Arapaho. In the sign language, Indians of the Great Plains designated the Atsina by a sweeping pass with both hands across the stomach, intended to convey the idea that they were beggars and always hungry. A similar gesture was used to designate the Hidatsa, the only difference being that the hands were moved across the body above the stomach, and this sign was meant to indicate that the Hidatsa men tattooed two parallel stripes across the chest. These stripes were shown in some picture writings. French traders evidently failed to notice the slight difference between the two gestures, and called the Atsina Big Bellies of the Prairie and the Hidatsa Big Bellies of the Missouri, and the identities prevailed long after the mistake was discovered by more careful observers.

Although they built permanent towns on or near the Missouri River, the Mandan and Hidatsa must be classed as semisedentary people. Through the coldest months of the winter, a large part of the population took refuge in sheltered woodland areas, which afforded plentiful supplies of fuel, and lived in small earth lodges which were easy to heat. In the spring the tribes would reassemble in the river towns. After the planting of crops, groups moved out on the Great Plains to hunt, using travois drawn by dogs (and later by horses) to carry their skin teepees and other equipment. The hunting, especially for the invaluable buffalo, continued until fall. Enough people remained in the towns to guard the fields and stored supplies against raiders, among whom were nomadic bands of their relatives, the Dakota Sioux.

The Missouri Valley towns of the Mandan and Hidatsa were strongly fortified by palisades and moats. The sites were chosen so that additional protection was gained from such natural features as steep bluffs and ravines. The circular lodges were large, some comfortably accommodating forty to fifty persons, and were constructed of heavy supporting timbers, wooden rafters and earth. The earthen roofs were dome-shaped, with a small flattened area at the top which contained a hole through which smoke from cooking and heating fires escaped. The entrance was a narrow passage, generally facing the East, and a skin curtain hung at each end. Most of the beds were against the outer wall, as were a horse corral, or stable, and storage pits for food, fodder and equipment, such as skin bullboats and farming tools. Some lodges were partially partitioned. Each contained a special place for the sacred medicine bundle of the occupants.

The Mandan and Hidatsa had matrilineal clan systems. Marriage between consanguineous relatives was prohibited. Among most people of the Great Plains brides were purchased, although this act did not make the girl a chattel of her husband. Lowie states that among the Mandan, however, "there was actually no purchase, but rather an exchange of gifts between the two families . . ." Both the Mandan and Hidatsa practiced polygamy, but most marriages were monogamous. "It was by no means degrading for a woman to be one of several wives," Lowie writes. "As a matter of fact, a man of distinction who married the eldest daughter in a family established a preemptive claim to her younger sisters as they reach maturity. . . . One reason for taking two or more wives was that a man of distinction owed it to his status to entertain, which in the absence of domestics involved considerable work for a single mate."

Pleas and obeisance to supernaturals were expressed in numerous ceremonials, some of them, notably the Sun Dance, involving the entire tribe and requiring weeks of preparation. The Mandan believed that every person had four souls, two living as spirits in some form of a hereafter, and two having functions on earth, after death.

Ever since physical descriptions of the Mandan were disseminated in the United States, they have been the subject of nonsensical theories voiced by religious groups. Their skin was fairer than that of most other Indians. The noses of most of them were thin and not so long and arched as those of other Great Plains people; some were aquiline or slightly curved, some short and straight, but none were broad. The men were tall, well-proportioned, broad-shouldered, muscular and vigorous. Some of the women were tall and robust.

With no more evidence than this on which to base their conclusions, various religious fanatics contrived a genesis for them. They were originally Spaniards, or they were Welshmen, or they were descendants of the Ten Lost Tribes of Israel. In any case, they were white Indians.

As sensible is the story which the Mandan themselves told of their origin. It was first obtained by interpreters with Lewis and Clark, who recorded it as follows:

> The whole nation resided in one large village underground near a subterraneous lake; a grapevine extended its roots down to their habitation and gave them a view of the light; some of the most adventurous climbed up the vine and were delighted with the sight of the earth, which they found covered with buffalo and rich with every kind of fruit; returning with the grapes they had gathered, their countrymen were so pleased with the taste of them that the whole nation resolved to leave their dull residence for the charms of the upper region; men, women, and children ascended by means of the vine; but when about half the nation had reached the surface of the earth, a corpulent woman who was clambering up the vine broke it with her weight, and closed upon herself and the rest of the nation the light of the sun.

The Mandan on earth always believed that with death they would return to the original underground dwelling place of their forefathers.

In 1733 the great trailbreaker and fur trader, Pierre Gaultier de Varennes, Sieur de La Vérendrye, was told by Cree and Assiniboin, with whom he was trading along the present Canadian boundary, of a large tribe of Indians who lived more than seven hundred miles to the southwest of the Lake of the Woods. Their eight villages stood on an immense river that ran toward the setting sun, and these people had large fields of corn, beans and pumpkins, besides unlimited quantities of hides and furs.

For five years La Vérendrye was prevented by other explorations and trading problems from going to find the people of the great western river, but in 1738 he reached the towns of the Mandan, Hidatsa and Arikara on the upper Missouri. This was the first recorded visit of a European to these tribes, although there is reason to believe that some unidentified French *voyageurs* had reached the river from Canada a few years earlier.

In the following century French, British and American fur traders appeared in the region each summer. The towns of the Hidatsa, Mandan and Arikara became important trading centers. The American period began about the time Lewis and Clark were returning down the Missouri from their expedition to the Pacific, and American posts were soon thereafter established at many places along the upper river. The American fur trade knew its greatest days in the early decades of the nineteenth century. The largest and richest organization engaged in this commerce was the American Fur Company, owned by John Jacob Astor of New York.

In the early summer of 1837, an American Fur Company steamboat, the *St. Peters*, left St. Louis heavily loaded with merchandise for the Indian trade. High officers of the company were passengers on the boat when several cases of smallpox were discovered. They had ample time to turn it back before reaching the upper Missouri, but to have done that would have meant the loss of the summer's trade. They might have unloaded the cargo, fumigated it and sent it on up the river in keelboats propelled by oars, shore draglines and sails, but to have done that would have meant an increase in the cost of operations and a decrease in profits. They did neither.

Carrying its uncontrolled pestilence, the *St. Peters* went on. The company officers stupidly attempted to keep Indians from coming near it. If they had commanded the sun not to rise, they would have had as much success. The Indians knew the boat carried supplies they badly needed, and they suspected that the efforts to keep them away were part of some scheme to cheat them. They swarmed about the boat, and virtually everything they touched sealed their doom.

On upstream the *St. Peters* steamed, spreading the deadly bane. Hundreds of Indians died each day in the summer of 1837. So many bodies were there in the villages and about the trading posts that it was impossible for those not stricken to bury them, and they were thrown into the river, over cliffs and into gullies. About most towns, posts and missions a terrible stench filled the air.

On each side of the river for five hundred miles, between Fort Pierre (South Dakota) and the mouth of the Yellowstone, Indian lodges stood but no smoke rose from them, no sounds of human life, except the wails and screams of the dying, broke the fearful silence. Brave Indian men killed themselves, unable to stand the sight of flesh rotting on their women and children.

More than fifteen thousand Indians were victims of the greed, the coldness, the criminal negligence of the American Fur Company officers.

Only thirty Mandan were still alive when the *St. Peters* went back down the river, loaded with furs which had been gathered at company posts. An exact figure for the losses of the Hidatsa is unavailable, but they suffered to a similar extent. Both tribes were virtually wiped out. Shortly afterward the little bands of survivors moved together to the Little Missouri River, near Fort Berthold, North Dakota, where eventually a reservation was set aside for them and other remnants of once proud river tribes.†

†The Fort Berthold Indian Agency and the cemeteries of the Mandan, Hidatsa and Arikara remnants were inundated with the completion of Garrison Dam and Garrison Lake, c. 1948, resulting in yet another move for these people to New Town, North Dakota, and an area to the west of the new lake.

4   There is no record to indicate with any degree of certainty
when the CROW separated from the Hidatsa. There is only
the tradition, shared by both groups, that they parted on the
upper Missouri River. Circumstantial evidence leads to the
belief that the division occurred in the eighteenth century,
but whether it was early or late in that period has not been
ascertained beyond reasonable doubt. Hayden suggests 1776
as an approximate date, but other ethnologists think it took
place considerably before that year. The first explorers and
the traders who followed them could learn nothing more
definite about the matter from either the Hidatsa or Crow.
Traditions lived for them, but chronology was of little
meaning, and was ignored or at best loosely expressed in the
stories they related about their own past.

But if it cannot be said when the Crow left the Hidatsa, it
is known why they departed and where they went. The
cause of the separation was a bitter wrangle between two
leaders of equal political influence which developed over a
division of spoils and authority. Diplomacy failed to resolve
the differences. One group remained on the Missouri, the
other set off into the West.

The people who would call themselves Crow crossed the
Great Plains and elected to settle in the shadow of the Rocky
Mountains. They may have had horses on their journey, but
if they did not, they soon acquired them. It is known that
horses had reached the northern Great Plains before the
seventeenth century.

The new homeland of the Crow was surrounded by enemy
tribes, among them the Sitsika (Blackfoot), the Dakota
Sioux, Arapaho, Atsina, Cheyenne, Shoshoni, Flathead and
Pawnee, all of whom wandered into the region on forays and
to hunt. From the time the Crow entered it no year passed
without warfare. However, the Crow were not always fighting as defenders. They were daring and vicious warriors, and
they raided other tribes, taking horses and scalps. One

factor gave them an advantage: If necessary they could retreat into mountain strongholds that were impregnable.

The Crow called themselves *Absaroke*, which means "bird people." To the French they were known as *gens des corbeaux*, and traders came to speak of their realm as *Absaroka*. It was a beautiful land rolling against the blue crystal wall of the Big Horn Mountains and the towering peaks of the Wind River Range. Over the sea of grass that swept away on every side from the Yellowstone, the Big Horn, the Powder, the Tongue, the Wind and other streams grazed immense herds of buffalo and other game valuable for food and hides, and the region was rich in beaver and otter and other furbearing animals.

When they lived in the Midwestern woodlands and on the Missouri River the Crow had been farmers, but when they migrated across the Great Plains they abandoned agriculture, and became a hunting and food-gathering people, depending entirely on the natural bounties of the land. The only crop they cultivated in Absaroka was tobacco, and this was done because it played an extraordinarily important part in their religion.

It is improbable that any people of the Great Plains possessed qualities and characteristics of greater variance, or more complicated social and political structures. They were physically strong and morally weak. They were highly intelligent and extremely superstitious.

The tribe maintained the matrilineal clan system, and contained numerous military, social and ceremonial groups and societies. Lowie, who made an exhaustive study of the Crow, states that the matrimonial history of a typical Crow man might "consist of several love matches and a single orthodox marriage by purchase, which through the sororate often became polygamous. A woman did not become an outcast by associating herself with a man from inclination: she merely fell short of ideal perfection. Indeed, she would not even rouse unfavorable comment unless she frequently changed mates. A handsome or brave man was expected to have an indefinite number of love affairs . . ." It might be noted, simply as a matter of interest, that because of their moral laxity the Crow were despised—and perhaps envied—by the Sioux and Cheyenne, who maintained generally strict moral codes.

Regarding the extreme superstitiousness of the Crow, Lowie notes:

Sometimes an inanimate object, because of its oddity, was treated as a "supernatural" person. A Crow who found a peculiarly shaped rock suggestive of an animal would treasure it, grease it, wrap it up with beads and other offerings, and believe it capable of reproduction. Periodically the owner would pray to the rock to grant him long life and wealth. . . . A Crow brave did not venture on a raid without the prompting of a supernatural protector in a dream or vision. . . . A Crow usually cut off a finger joint of his left hand or in some way mortified his flesh by way of arousing supernatural pity.

The elders of many tribes regularly prompted their children to seek a revelation, but Lowie writes that "no such admonition was customary among the Crow. There a lad grew up, constantly hearing that all success in life was derived from visions; hence, being eager for horses and for social recognition, an adolescent would go out to fast, praying for rich booty, for a chance to strike a *coup* or for some other benefit. A mature man or woman would seek a vision whenever a special cause arose—if his children were sick, if he had lost his property, if he longed to revenge the killing of a close relative, and so on."

Terrell wrote of the Crow (1971) that "they sought to avoid white men, despising them and their ways of life. They were horse thieves *par excellence*, and would plunder whenever an opportunity arose. They were inordinately vain. The men wore their hair long and took great pride in caring for it. As craftsmen they ranked with the finest of the Great Plains, showing talent as well as taste in the products they manufactured. Their bows were large and beautiful, some of them covered with rattlesnake skin or decorated with colorful designs." The women were extremely skillful in making clothing and leather goods. Their shirts and dresses of tanned bighorn sheepskin, and their buffalo robes, embroidered and ornamented with dyed porcupine quills, were particularly handsome.

Among the Crow there was no such thing as an orphan. Indeed, the greatest insult a person could hurl at another was to accuse him or her of having no relatives. Parentless children were adopted by adults of the sib to which they had been born and were shown great affection. The tribe was divided into thirteen exogamous mother-sibs, but personal names were in no way connected with sib names. Usually a young person was given a name deriving from a characteristic, an experience or a deed.

Corporal punishment was rare or mild among the Crow, but they had a strong psychological deterrent to wrongdoing. It was applied by persons called "joking relatives." A Crow's joking relative was either his father's brother's child or his father's male sib mate's child. "Although the accusations leveled by joking relatives against each other were often groundless," states Driver, "the threat of one's protagonist finding real holes in the armor of his personality was always present and served as a deterrent to defiant behavior."

The Crow not only loved their children and cared for them in every possible way, but guided them with gentleness and intelligence. Rarely were they scolded or criticized in public. According to Driver, the family and sib presented a "united front to the outside and sought to protect and defend their members rather than to ridicule them." Young persons were rewarded for deeds well done, and even when they had tried to succeed in an undertaking but had failed. Blaming a person for an honest mistake or an unavoidable failure was considered inadvisable as well as unbeneficial.

To the Crow the tobacco plant had a sacred character. Two kinds were raised, one for ordinary smoking and the other, called medicine tobacco, to be smoked only on special occasions and in religious rites. The Crow Tobacco Society was unique and its ceremonies were among the most colorful performed by any Great Plains people. J. D. McGuire writes (in Hodge) that the observances in the planting of medicine tobacco included "a solemn march, a foot race among the young men, the planting of seed, the building of a hedge of green branches around the seed bed, a visit to the sweat house, followed by a bath and a solemn smoke, all ending with a feast." When the tobacco was ripe, it was harvested with more ceremonies and social activities. The leafs were stored in specially constructed shelters, and the seeds were put into deerskin pouches, to be kept for the next planting season. As a gesture of thankfulness to the patron spirit of the tobacco plant, some of the leaves and seeds were cut and crushed into tiny fragments and dropped into a flowing creek, to be carried away to the realm of the gods.

The identities of the first Europeans to meet the Crow in their far western homeland are unknown. Although they were almost constantly at war with other tribes, according to tradition, they made strenuous efforts to avoid serious clashes with whites. History gives Lewis and Clark credit for finding them first in their historic empire, but it would be safe to wager—if it could be proven—that French *voyageurs* were in the Yellowstone and Big Horn region at an earlier time. Pointing toward such an assumption is the fact that as late as the 1930s old Crows used the expression *Beta-awka-wahcha* for white men, meaning "Sits-on-the water," i.e., trappers traveling by canoe. These Indians maintained that the phrase referred to early Frenchmen and not to Americans, such as Lewis and Clark. Of course, they could not have remembered events of 1804, but knew the meaning of the term by tradition. In speaking of Americans the Crows borrowed an expression from the Cheyenne, who called all whites "yellow-eyes" —*Masta-chuda* in the Crow tongue—thus making a definite distinction between early French *voyageurs*, or fur hunters, and American explorers and trappers.

The Crow are still there, in Absaroka.

5 Sometime in the first third of the seventeenth century, French missionaries and traders heard from Indians in the Lake Huron region about a strong people who dwelt in a land of great forests and many streams far to the west beyond large inland seas. The best that French ears could do with the name of these people, as they heard it from the Chippewa and other Algonquian tribes, was *Nadouessioux*, and this soon became *Scioux* and then *Sioux*.

Distorted in the form *Naduesiu*, the name was first recorded in the Jesuit Relations of 1640, but that was several years after it was known, and twenty years before any European would meet the Indians to whom it was applied. These Indians were the four tribes comprising the Santee Sioux, the MDEWKANTON, WAHPETON, WAPEKUTE and SISSETON. In their homeland, which would become the state of Minnesot᷒, were the headwaters of the greatest of all rivers of the continent, the Mississippi.

It is probable that the Mdewkanton were the main stem from which the other three tribes of the Santee division developed. Traditions of these people relate that at some remote period they drifted southward into Minnesota from Canada, north of Lake Superior. They may always have been Northern Woodland Indians, living entirely by hunting and food gathering. They were still following this mode of life at the beginning of the historical period. However, when they had established themselves in Minnesota after their migration from the North—if it took place—they were in touch with other people who lived much farther south, and their culture began to undergo changes.

Archaeology has determined that the Santee were in the Mille Lacs area of Minnesota as early as A.D. 1300. Yet, it is known that Indians were in central and western Minnesota in the Archaic period, perhaps ten to twelve thousand years ago, for bones have been found to which scientists ascribe this great antiquity. Whether or not these ancient people were ancestral to the northern Siouans cannot, of course, be known, for they left nothing—at least nothing has been found—to connect them with their descendants, but some evidence indicates they were not entirely isolated.

In 1930 a road was being cut through a gravel deposit, some ten feet below ground surface, near Pelican Rapids. A grader operator's eyes were attracted by a shiny white object, and he stopped work to pick it up. It appeared to be part of a shell. Next he saw that nearby some bones were exposed. A little digging by hand resulted in the recovery of a human skull and part of a skeleton.

In this way one of the most important archaeological finds in America was made. Scientists, summoned to the site, at first thought the bones and skull were those of a young male, but further examination left no doubt that they had belonged to a young female, probably no more than fifteen years of age.

With the remains was a knife about nine inches in length which had been made from an antler. Even more important, as far as the archaeologists were concerned, was part of a perforated shell that lay among the ribs and vertebrae of the abdominal area, and which she probably had worn as a pendant on a thong. The shell was identified as a species found on the Gulf of Mexico. Obviously, since she had it in her possession, there must have been contact between Paleo-Indians of Minnesota and people living farther to the south. The most reasonable assumption is that it reached Minnesota through trade channels.

The artifacts were of great interest, but it was the location in which the skeleton had been found that created excitement in the scientific world. The gravel through which the road cut was being made was the bed of an ancient body of water, called Glacial Lake Pelican, which had formed shortly after the retreat of the last continental ice sheet, perhaps some twenty thousand years ago, and several millennia later had become extinct. The varved clay from which the remains and artifacts had been extracted belonged to the Pleistocene, and had been laid down some eleven thousand years ago. Was the girl interred in a grave ten feet deep? That is not a reasonable assumption. The suggestion that she was buried in a landslide is not substantiated by the geology of the site. Even if she had fallen or had been buried in an open pit ten feet deep, it would be necessary to conclude that the crack had closed over without crushing or disturbing the bones, a most unlikely occurrence. If, by some remote chance, that had happened, the girl's skeleton would still belong to the Pleistocene, for according to the noted archaeologist, Wormington, the special climatic and topographic "conditions necessary to induce landsliding would be associated with a period almost as remote as the varve formation" in which the bones were found.

While there has been a great deal of scientific squabbling over the age and fate of the Pleistocene girl, most geologists and archaeologists are inclined to believe that she met death by some form of accident.

Within the next five years the skeletal remains of two Pleistocene men were recovered at Brown's Valley and West Union, Minnesota. These sites were in gravel deposits associated with Glacial Lake Agassiz. No firm date has been assigned to these remains, but it is significant that with the bones recovered at Brown's Valley archaeologists found projectile points known to be eight thousand years old and similar to others uncovered in a site in Wyoming.

In the early centuries of the Christian Era one of America's most unique cultural developments occurred in the Minnesota area. There is reason to think that Siouans may have created it. Many types of wooden, bone and flint weapons, utensils and ornaments were supplanted by articles made of copper. In surface nuggets and exposed deposits the copper lay in almost pure form near the shores of Lake Superior. The richest deposits were on the Keweenaw Peninsula of northern Michigan and on Isle Royal.

The copper pounders—they knew nothing of smelting—were the first metalworkers of North America, possibly the first in the world.

At first they worked with the copper as they had worked with the stones from which they made their projectile points, that is, they pecked it and flaked it. Soon, however, the peculiar qualities of the metal impressed their acute minds, and they found that they could shape it into almost any article they desired by pounding.

The influences and products of the Old Copper Culture rapidly spread through the Midwestern and Eastern United States region, and even southward into Mexico. Tools, ornaments, weapons and utensils made of Lake Superior copper have been recovered in Florida, Ohio, Alabama, New England and on the Great Plains.

Archaeologists are unable to explain the rather sudden decline of the Old Copper Culture. Some scientists lean toward the conclusion that its end was brought about by changing religious ritual and burial customs. This seems to be a logical explanation, for the Old Copper Culture appears to have been absorbed by the Effigy Mound Culture, which was certainly of Siouan origin in the northern woodlands region.

Martin writes that the Old Copper Culture "seems to have been related to the Black Sand Culture of Illinois as well as to the pre-pottery cultures in Illinois." He and his colleagues give A.D. 700 as a terminal date for the Old Copper Culture. Of the ancient Black Sand Culture, Hyde states that Siouan Indian Knoll people "established the Black Sand center," and that the Black Sand folk had cultural traits "from the Tennessee River Indian Knoll centers at Eva in west Tennessee and at Lauderdale in northern Alabama."

The Siouan Effigy Mound Culture, as previously stated, spread from Wisconsin into Illinois, Iowa and Minnesota. Although they knew how to grow crops, the Effigy Mound people are believed to have been incipient farmers, depending for the greater part of their sustenance on hunting, fishing and gathering wild plant foods, especially the wild rice which grew in abundance in the Wisconsin-Minnesota area.

The Santee already occupied eastern Minnesota when the dramatic, colorful religious ritual and burial customs of the Mound Builder faith, out of which the Effigy Mound Culture developed, reached them. In this early period, as they depended on the natural bounties of the forests, lakes and marshes for their survival, they continued to be wandering bands and did not establish large permanent villages adjacent to agricultural projects. "Wandering about in small camps the greater part of the year," Hyde writes, "they exposed the dead, probably on scaffolds raised on tall poles. When the flesh decayed, they cleaned the bones and made neat bundles of them, which they carried about from camp to camp." In the spring, all the bands met at a rendezvous, agreed upon in the previous fall. The high point of the spring gathering was the Feast of the Dead, and Hyde declares that this important ceremonial "was obviously the Sioux version of the Mound Builder burial ceremonies."

Hundreds of years later, the first white men to meet the Santee Sioux in eastern Minnesota were guests in the spring Feast of the Dead. They were the explorer-traders Médart Chouart, Sieur de Groseilliers, and his brother-in-law, Pierre Esprit Radisson. After a terrible winter in northern Wisconsin, during which they nearly starved to death, they pushed westward to the headwater streams of the Mississippi in the early spring of 1660.

For very good reasons, the Santee were eager to develop a trade with the French. Tribes to the northeast had been for some years previously receiving French goods and weapons, giving them a decided advantage, not only with an improved economy but on the field of battle. The Santee, still armed with spears and bows and arrows, could not stand before the onslaughts of enemies with firearms. Therefore, when the Santee learned that Radisson and Groseilliers were not a great distance away they sent ambassadors, heavily laden with food and other gifts, to invite them to the annual rendezvous.

The meeting apparently was a great success. Although the exact site of it is not known, it marked the beginning of the historical period for the Santee and possibly other Siouan groups.*

The Santee were in their historic Minnesota homelands when the American period began for them with the upper Mississippi expedition in 1805 of Lieut. Zebulon M. Pike. Pike's mission was to prepare the way for the ousting of British traders operating on United States soil. As far as accomplishments were concerned, his journey was largely a fiasco, and his reports were inaccurate. It might be said, however, that Pike's presence among the Santee marked the opening of their road to ruin.

After years of ill-treatment from both westward-moving settlers and both the local and federal governments, in July, 1851, the Wahpeton and Sisseton ceded to the United States their lands in southern and western Minnesota, as well as some in Iowa and Dakota. "The price for this magnificent empire," writes Carley, "was $1,665,000 in cash and annuities." In August of the same year, the Mdewkanton and Wahpekute signed away their territorial claims, which embraced most of the southeast quarter of Minnesota. The government agreed to pay them $1,410,000 in cash and annuities over a fifty-year period.

In all, the Santee ceded about twenty-four million acres of rich timber and agricultural lands. Left for their use were two relatively small reservations, each about twenty miles wide and seventy miles long, through which flowed the upper Minnesota River. It soon became apparent that there were unforeseen "loopholes" in the 1851 treaties. According to Carley, the Santee charged that they had been tricked into signing "a traders' paper which had never been explained to them. It gave to traders and half-breeds for claims against the Indians some four hundred thousand dollars, which would otherwise have been paid to the tribes in cash."

Storm clouds continued to gather. Grafting agents, most of whom

---

*Although they bear the same name, no means have been found to connect the Santee Sioux of South Carolina with the Santee Sioux of Minnesota, either through language or archaeology. It might be noted, however, that the burial customs and ritual of the two widely separated tribes were similar in many respects.

knew nothing about Indians and all of whom were political appointees, continued to allow annuities to flow into the coffers of traders. Honest and hardworking agents struggled to train the Santee as farmers and craftsmen, so that they might support themselves and gradually be absorbed in the pattern of civilization. They met with little success, chiefly for two reasons: Most of the Santee demanded that they be allowed to maintain their old fishing and hunting culture, in which agriculture played a very small part, and more often than not the farming equipment, seeds and blacksmithing and carpentering tools promised by the treaties did not arrive; nor did food stores the government had agreed to supply them each summer materialize, a large part of them being stolen by crooked contractors and their cohorts in the Indian Bureau.

Within a few years after the signing of the treaties of 1851, the two reservations were completely surrounded by white farmers, and many more were demanding that the Santee lands be drastically reduced. The government responded by taking a number of Santee leaders to Washington, where they were pressured into relinquishing their claim along the north side of the Minnesota River, in total about a million acres, for which they were to be paid an amount to be fixed by the United States Senate. The Santee leaders went home and waited two years, but the payment did not come. At last the Senate decided that thirty cents an acre was a fair price. There was nothing the Santee could do. When the money finally was appropriated, they got only about half of it, the other half going to settle the claims of traders, many of which were totally fraudulent.

The winter of 1861–1862 was one of near starvation for the Santee. In desperate condition, they looked forward to June, when goods and cash annuities were due to be given them. Nothing came in June. Nothing came in July. Nothing came in August. Purportedly the payments that would save them were held up by Treasury officials who could not agree whether to issue paper money or coin.

Meanwhile, in July, some five thousand Santee descended on the Upper Minnesota Agency. They surrounded two companies of troops stationed there, holding them in their barracks while warriors looted the government warehouse, which contained a large quantity of stores. Bloodshed was averted by the commanding officer, who kept his head, and made arrangements for the Indians to receive the food they so desperately needed.

The storm temporarily subsided, but rapidly regathered its strength, and broke in full fury on Sunday, August 17, 1862. The Santee went on the warpath. Led by Little Crow, they swept upon settlements and farms.

Before the uprising could be brought under control by federal troops and armed bands of civilians, at least 700 white settlers and 100 soldiers had been slain. The burned ruins of buildings marked the Minnesota countryside, and the carcasses of livestock rotted in countless pastures. Indian casualties were not tabulated, but they were heavy.

Some Santee fled westward, finding refuge among the Dakota of the Great Plains, and others went to Canada. Chief Little Crow was ambushed by civilians. His body was scalped and otherwise mutilated, then buried in a pile of offal. Thirty-nine other leaders were captured by soldiers and condemned to death. One, named Round Wind, was pardoned by Pres. Abraham Lincoln. All the others were hanged.

The remaining Santee, numbering several thousand, were held in concentration camps. Their reservation was taken from them and opened to white settlement.*

In March, 1863, Congress authorized President Lincoln to set apart for the Santee "a reserve beyond the limits of any State and remove them thereto." Under military guard, they were taken to the new "homeland" selected for them in Dakota Territory.

*See Part Five, Chap. 1, about the Winnebago of Minnesota.

6   In the sixteenth and seventeenth centuries, Minnesota and immediately adjacent areas were dominated by people who were unquestionably of Siouan stock. Long before the French in Canada had heard of them they were divided into distinct tribes. Some of them undoubtedly had drifted to the northern woodlands from the Ohio Valley region, perhaps from Kentucky and Tennessee, but the early migrations of others must remain in the realm of pure conjecture. While it is not inconceivable that Siouan groups dwelt on the headwaters of the Mississippi several thousand years ago, in that remote age designated by scientists as the Archaic period, there is a tendency to favor the theory that they began to infiltrate the far northern woodlands of the United States at a much later time, perhaps shortly before or shortly after the beginning of the Christian Era, and that the direction of their movements was from south to north, and afterward toward the west. Therefore, through an unknown number of millenniums, they must have passed over a great circular route, the western perimeter of which may have been, and probably was, the eastern slope of the Canadian and American Rocky Mountains.

If it cannot be known when the YANKTON, YANKTONAI, HUNKPATINA and ASSINIBOIN reached northern Minnesota or whence they came—they were at one time consanguineously, culturally and linguistically a distinct branch of the immense Siouan family—it can be stated unequivocally that they were there many years before any of their names were heard by Europeans. Even before they had any contact with whites, a major division in their ranks had occurred, and it would evolve into a significant chapter in Siouan history.

In studying the spiritual beliefs, ceremonies and other religious practices of the various subdivions of the Dakota Sioux one would find them strikingly similar. The cosmology of the Yankton and Yanktonai branches conformed to the general pattern. Science and religion could not be separated, for they were one. In the divine hierarchy of the Sioux were many gods and spirits, making their existence known in countless ways, but all were embodied in, and subservient to, a supreme being, Wakan Tanka, the Great Mystery.

Wankan Tanka, writes Hassrick, "is the Chief God, the Great Spirit, the Creator, and the Executive. He is the Gods both Superior and Associate and he is the Gods-Kindred. . . . He is the good and evil gods, the visible and invisible, the physical and immaterial for He is all in one.

"The gods had no beginning and they will have no ending. . . . Since the gods were created, not born, they will not die. Mankind cannot fully understand these things, for they are of the Great Mystery."

Some ethnologists think that fear of the dead was not deeply ingrained in the Sioux psychology. This seems to be a generalization that, in the interest of accuracy, requires some qualification. Many Siouans, especially elderly men and women, made a practice of avoiding burial sites and told terrifying ghost stories to youngsters to keep them away from such places. However, it was a custom of the bereaved of some Siouan tribes to visit cemeteries on formal occasions. On these pilgrimages, usually undertaken if possible on the anniversary of a death, gifts of food or other tokens were placed on graves to placate the spirits of the dead, and efforts were made by words or thoughts to assure the departed that they had not been forgotten and love for them still lived.

Speaking specifically of the Assiniboin, the famous missionary-explorer De Smet wrote:

> They bind the bodies with thongs of rawhide between the branches of large trees, and, more frequently, place them on scaffolds, to protect them from the wolves and other wild animals. They are higher than a man can reach. The feet are always turned to the west. There they are left to decay. When the scaffolds or the trees to which the dead are attached fall, through age, the relatives bury all the other bones, and place the skulls in a circle in the plain, with the faces turned toward the center. They preserve these with care, and consider them objects of religious veneration. You will generally find there several bison skulls. In the center stands the medicine poke, about twenty feet high, to which *Wah-Kons* are hung, to guard and protect the sacred deposit. The Indians call the cemetery the village of the dead. They visit it at certain seasons of the year, to converse affectionately with their deceased relatives and friends, and always leave some present.

Like other Dakota Sioux, the Yankton and Yanktonai groups

believed that every person had four souls, three of which died with the body. "The fourth," states Underhill, "could be kept for a while by a loving family in the form of a 'spirit bundle.'" The bundle would contain some small personal article owned by the deceased—in the case of a child perhaps a lock of hair—carefully wrapped in valuable skins and kept off the ground by a tripod. According to Underhill, "all the camp brought gifts to the soul, which were stored up toward the day of its final release." When that day came, a solemn ritual was observed. It included the offering of smoke to the Great Mystery on behalf of all the creatures of the earth, and the consuming of certain foods by young women who were virgins.

"For the Sioux," Hassrick comments, "a reverent acceptance of man's rightful place presupposed an understanding of the universe. Knowledge and interpretation of natural forces became the science of living essential to the very existence of the individual . . . this search for understanding was a national concept. It did not result in skepticism but led to the development of highly systematic beliefs in the universal forces and the supernatural." It is his opinion that the candid acknowledgment of the Sioux that their concepts "did not fully answer all the questions which man's curiosity and wonder are capable of posing, that certain truths are beyond comprehension and must be accepted on faith, shows the maturity of Sioux thinking, the subtlety of Sioux theology."

There is no doubt that both the Hunkpatina and the Assiniboin were originally divisions of the Yanktonai, but whether this is true of the Yankton as well has never been satisfactorily determined, and neither early nor late records throw much light on the question. The Assiniboin are mentioned in the Jesuit Relations of 1640 as a distinct tribe. Obviously, therefore, they must have parted at an earlier time from the Yanktonai. Some ethnologists place the date of the separation at the beginning of the seventeenth century, but others believe that it occurred at an earlier time.

The first mention of the Yankton was by Father Louis Hennepin, who was a captive of the Sioux in 1680. He placed them north of Mille Lacs in the vicinity of Leech and Red lakes, Minnesota. The name Yanktonai did not appear in records until considerably later. Dr. Cyrus Thomas (in Hodge) declares that "although the name Yankton was known earlier than Yanktonai, it does not follow that the Yankton were the elder tribe . . . the name Yankton and some of its synonyms appear early to have been used to include the two tribes, the distinction probably not then being known." This apparently was the case for considerably more than a century after Hennepin's time.

As for the Hunkpatina, they were always in close association with the Yanktonai. The first reference to them appeared in the journals of Lewis and Clark in 1804, and they were then living below the Yanktonai on the James River in eastern South Dakota. This location resulted in the name Lower Yanktonai being applied to them by fur traders.

All four tribes being considered in this part eventually became Great Plains Indians. The first to leave their traditional northern Minnesota homeland were the Assiniboin. Parting from the Yanktonai, they moved northward into Canada and became closely associated with the Cree. This shift probably was prompted by a strong determination to improve their economy. No reports have been found indicating that the separation was caused by irreconcilable political or religious differences. On the other hand, tribes north of the Great Lakes were obtaining French goods and weapons, if not directly then through Indian intermediaries or middlemen, that were transported over the water routes connecting Canadian areas with the St. Lawrence River. The Assiniboin's alliance with the Algonquian Cree was never abrogated.

One of the largest and most powerful Siouan tribes, the Assiniboin spread during the seventeenth and eighteenth centuries over an enormous region embracing territory in both Canada and the United States. Early traders and missionaries found groups of them scattered from north of Lake Winnipeg to the Missouri River, from James Bay on the east to the Rocky Mountains on the west. The establishment of British posts on Hudson Bay provided them with an advantageous northern outlet for their furs. Later they also traded at upper Missouri River posts.

Ironically they eventually became deadly enemies of other Siouan tribes of the northern Great Plains, especially the Teton Dakota, with whom they were almost constantly at war until forced onto reservations by both the Canadian and American governments. Before this long and bloody conflict developed, however, they enjoyed a relatively peaceful existence. In the Canadian wilderness that reached northward from the Lake of the Woods and Lake Nipigon to the Arctic wastes, Kennedy writes that they thrived, and "rattled like peas in a giant pod, living almost in a vacuum in their vast realm. Far to the east were the Iroquois, seen only rarely by a far-ranging war party; far to the west were the Blackfeet—and probably even their most adventuresome respective war parties had not yet made contact. Only the peaceful, orderly Crees and Chippewas lived within this vast circle; and, since their campsites were quite stable, the Assiniboines lived in and around them, like a giant grizzly who roams undisturbed among the other wildlife, large and small, in the wilderness."

The meaning of names:
Yankton—*End Village.*
Yanktonai—*Little-end Village.*
Hunkpatina—*Campers at the End of the Circle.*
Assiniboin—*One Who Cooks with the Use of Stones.*

Numerous white men who saw the Assiniboin in their greatest years, in both Canada and the United States, speak of them as being among the finest human specimens of all the northern aborigines. They were distinguished not only for their physical prowess but for their cunning, courage and capabilities as warriors, for their innate intelligence and for their enterprise as producers and traders. The noted authorities, Mooney and Thomas, write (in Hodge): "As they have lived since the appearance of the whites in the northwest almost wholly on the plains, without permanent villages, moving from place to place in search of food, their history has been one of conflict with surrounding tribes." Not only northern Siouans were their enemies; they fought, aided by the Cree, the Siksika (Blackfeet) for control of the western Canadian and northern Montana plains and are known to have crossed the Rocky Mountains to raid the Kutenai, Salish and other groups.

Assiniboin men, according to Mooney and Thomas, dressed their hair in various ways, but it was seldom cut. As it grew it was twisted into small locks or tails, and frequently false hair was added to lengthen the twist until it reached the ground. In warfare and probably during buffalo hunts the long hair was coiled on top of the head. The British explorer, Alexander Henry, called the Assiniboin the most expert buffalo hunters on the northern Great Plains, and the greatest producers and traders of pemmican. Traders often remarked about their extraordinary hospitality. By the time they had become full-fledged Plains people, their dress, tepees and customs resembled more those of the Plains Cree than of the Dakota Sioux. They are said to have sacrificed dogs to their deities. Their greatest ceremonial, as was the case with most Plains tribes, was the Sun Dance, usually held in the early summer. Unlike other tribes, however, the Assiniboin, as Kennedy states, "did not associate self-torture with the Sun Dance. It was used only in preparation for war. . . . Braves who aspired to lead a war party often lay out in the rain or snow for several nights, fasting and praying to the Great Spirit for favorable visions; and some of them gashed their arms and breasts with knives, the more to excite his pity." The Assiniboin acquired horses early in the eighteenth century, and they became daring and expert horse thieves. Oddly, however, they continued to use dogs as beasts of burden long after they might have become fully mounted Indians and have traveled with horse-drawn instead of dog-drawn travois.

Although the Assiniboin were famed as warriors and fought incessantly with other tribes, white men had extremely little trouble with them. From the time of their discovery, through the long period of the fur trade, and even for years after settlers began to occupy their vast Great Plains domain, they strived to maintain friendly relations with the invaders. No United States troops, as Kennedy notes, "were ever needed against them." Yet, it was the whiskey, the diseases and the injustices of Americans that brought about their final destruction. In 1836, according to an Indian Bureau report issued in 1843, a smallpox epidemic took the lives of four thousand Assiniboin men, women and children. After the disastrous wars with the Sioux (in which the Assiniboin took no part), the federal government established two reserves in Montana, at Fort Belknap and Fort Peck. There the remnants of the once great Assiniboin tribe still struggling to survive in the American West—numbering only about two thousand—were assigned permanent homes.

Near the end of the seventeenth century, the Yanktonai apparently began to move westward from their old homeland north of Mille Lacs, while the Yankton migrated toward the southwest. The Yanktonai (and the Hunkpatina) may have accompanied the Teton Dakota or have followed their course a short time later. It is believed that the Yanktonai stopped on the Red River for some time, later hunting, or possibly dwelling, as far west as the James River. For approximately a hundred years their name did not appear in records, although they evidently were in this area of North and South Dakota. Notice of them was taken by Lewis and Clark in 1804, and these explorers wrote that they roved over a large area embracing the headwaters of the Sioux,

James and Red rivers. They had strong bonds with British traders, and reportedly sent warriors to fight Americans in the War of 1812.

The American explorer, Maj. Stephen H. Long, reported that in 1819 the Yanktonai were one of the most important Dakota tribes and hunted from the Red River of the North as far west as the Missouri River. For purposes of trade they visited numerous Northern posts. According to Long, they had no fixed residence, but wandered over the plains east of the Missouri, dwelling "in fine lodges of well-dressed and decorated skins." Long described one Yanktonai chieftain as wearing

> a splendid cloak of buffalo skins, dressed so as to be a fine white color, which was decorated with tufts of owl feathers and others of various hues. His necklace was formed of about 60 claws of the grizzly bear, and his leggings, jacket, and moccasins were of white skins profusely decorated with human hair, the moccasins being variegated with plumage from several birds. In his hair, secured by a strip of red cloth, he wore 9 sticks neatly cut and smoothed and painted with vermillion, which designated the number of gunshot wounds he had received. His hair was plaited in two tresses, which hung forward; his face was painted with vermillion, and in his hand he carried a large fan of turkey feathers.

Both the Yanktonai and the Hunkpatina must have been recognized as strong tribes and feared warriors, for Dr. Cyrus Thomas wrote that in 1865 separate treaties of peace were made with the United States "binding them to use their influence and power to prevent hostilities not only against citizens, but also between the Indian tribes in the region occupied or frequented by them."

Apparently, however, the pacts did not inspire them to make strenuous efforts in behalf of people who were taking their lands and killing off the game on which they depended, and warfare continued to rage across this region of the northern Great Plains. Subsequently, United States troops rounded up the Yanktonai and Hunkpatina, and forced them onto reservations in the Dakotas and Montana, thus breaking them up into groups that could be controlled with comparative ease.

About the year 1708, the Yankton were on the east bank of the Missouri River, near the present Sioux City. Then, like the Yanktonai, for nearly a century they dropped almost entirely from history under their own name, there being scarcely any notice of them except as included under the general term Sioux. However, during this hundred years, and most probably for a longer time, they had been wandering over southwestern Minnesota and eastern Iowa, after drifting south from their northern Minnesota homeland. Early French reports not only make it clear that these people were Yanktons, but they drove other Siouans southward and westward. Ponca, Omaha, Iowa and Oto traditions all relate that they were attacked by the Yanktons. Hyde notes that the French explorer, Jean Francois le Seur, in 1700 called the Yankton the "Village of the Red Rock," meaning the famed pipestone quarry in extreme southwestern Minnesota, and "in later times the other Sioux admitted the right of the Yankton to control the quarry by right of discovery and occupation." At least, if the Yankton didn't discover this most valuable asset—and there is good reason to believe they did not—they took it by aggression and for some time profited from it.

After their long absence from history under their own name, Lewis and Clark restored them to their rightful place as a distinct tribe. Lewis wrote that they roamed along the James, Big and Little Sioux, Floyd and Des Moines rivers, an area which included the pipestone quarry. The Lewis and Clark journals describe them as being large, well proportioned, "and exhibiting a certain air of dignity and boldness." They trafficked extensively with American traders along the Missouri, and were generally friendly. They were, however, dangerous and bold warriors, and made bloody raids for booty against other Missouri River tribes.

Their friendliness toward Americans was dramatically demonstrated at the time of the Santee outbreak in Minnesota in 1862. The Yankton head chief, Palaneapape, prevented his warriors from joining the uprising. Dr. Thomas writes that he also sent a warning to white settlers in Dakota to flee to the forts, "thereby saving hundreds of lives."

A Yankton reservation was established in South Dakota, but the federal government's agents made no effort to differentiate between the Yankton and the Yanktonai. The Yankton tribe was splintered, some mixed with Yanktonai, and some forced to live with other Siouan groups on several reservations in both North and South Dakota.

7   The western trails of the Teton Sioux spread out across the immense rolling grass sea of the northern plains like seven tines of an inconceivably great fork. The handle of the fork was strangely crooked. Beginning in the region of Mille Lacs, not far from the western extremity of Lake Superior, it twisted southward, then turned toward the northwest, bent toward the southwest after passing the Red River, and reached the prongs at the upper Missouri River.

Farthest north, along the Knife and Cannonball rivers, southwest of the Mandan, went the HUNKPAPA, the SANS ARCS and the SIHASAPA (Blackfoot Band). Directly south of them were the MINICONJOU, along Grand River, and directly east of the Miniconjou were the OOHENONPA, or "Two Kettles." Farthest south were the Brulé. West of all were the OGLALA.

Far behind them all in the last quarter of the seventeenth century was Mille Lacs—some scholars believe their westward migration started at an earlier time—and some fifty years later they had crossed the upper Missouri. If one might think that it took them a long time to travel this distance, in reality, under the circumstances, the shift was accomplished with an almost remarkable swiftness. For they not only had to live as they moved, stopping to hunt and gather seasonal wild foods and provide themselves with sustenance and security for the long winters, but they had to overcome and drive off enemies who attacked and attempted to block their passage. It should be remembered as well that they had no definite goals; and they did not know the country that reached out to horizons on every side of them. Astonishing is the fact that almost within half a century the seven groups of the Teton Sioux were transposed from typical Woodland people into Indians fully capable of living, surviving and prospering in a totally different environment, the world of the Great Plains.

TETON SIOUX CALENDAR

JANUARY—The Moon of Popping Trees (Split with Cold)

FEBRUARY—The Moon of Sore Eyes (Snow Blindness)

MARCH—The Moon When the First Grain (Plants) Come Up

APRIL—The Moon of the Birth of (Bison) Calves

MAY—The Moon of Strawberries

JUNE—The Moon of Ripe Berries

JULY—The Moon of Chokecherries Ripening

AUGUST—The Moon of Ripe Plums

SEPTEMBER—The Moon of Calves Growing Black (also, The Moon of Yellow Leaves)

OCTOBER—The Moon of Falling Leaves

NOVEMBER—The Moon of Hairless Calves (fetuses found in slain bison cows)

DECEMBER—The Moon of Frost in the Tepee

The Dakota Teton always have been, and always will be, the "picture Indians" of western history. They fully deserve the distinction. Physically, mentally and morally they rank among the highest type of American Indians, and they are superior in these qualities to many tribes. As a warrior society they may not be compared to any other Indian peoples, with the possible exception of the Iroquois. As to courage and bravery they have no peers. As to color and beauty in their regalia, and complexity and drama in the social and religious ceremonials and ritual, they are unsurpassed. As to cohesiveness and unity as a people, as to faith in themselves as individuals, as to confidence in their capability to overcome all obstacles, all adversities, all enemies, and as egotists, they are incomparable.

That is, they were all of these things long before, and for much more than a century after, white men came to know them in their realms on the northern Great Plains. These admirable characteristics are not entirely dead in them, but Americans have succeeded in quenching them to faintly smouldering embers.

By the middle of the eighteenth century the Teton controlled all the country between the Missouri River and the Black Hills, the Little Missouri and the North Platte rivers. Although the groups were widely dispersed over this gigantic area, the bonds linking them strengthened instead of weakening. They wanted to meet in joint council each summer, but that was seldom possible, even after they had obtained horses in great numbers, for many exigencies arose to disrupt well-made plans. Seldom a summer passed, however, without some groups meeting, and there were years when large delegations from all seven tribes assembled. The annual gatherings were grand occasions, both solemn and gay. Leaders settled problems that were important to all. There were feasts and festivities, ceremonials and games, and the culmination of the celebration was the greatest of all Sioux rituals, the Sun Dance.

In both matters physical and spiritual *four* was the magic, or controlling, number. It was a concept early explained and understood, and to the Sioux logical beyond question.

Wakan Tanka was the Great Mystery, and he was endowed with four titles. As Hassrick, an authority on the Teton Sioux, states: "He was the Chief God, the Great Spirit, the Creator, and the Executive." Hassrick further defines the hierarchy of the gods as containing three other groups, each composed of four members, and ranking below Wakan Tanka in the order of Superior Gods, Gods-Kindred, and Gods-like. Yet the Great Mystery was all of these, for He was "the visible and the invisible, the physical and immaterial . . . sixteen in one, yet only one."

There were four directions. There were four elements above the earth: the sky, the sun, the moon, the stars. There were four parts of time: the day, the night, the month, the year. There were four phases of man's life: infancy, childhood, maturity, old age. There were four parts to all plants: roots, stem, leaves, fruit. There were four classes of animals: crawling, flying, two-legged, four-legged.

And so there were four virtues which all men were expected to seek: bravery, fortitude, generosity and wisdom. Hassrick writes:

While it was understood that no man could achieve excellence in all these qualities, it was believed that every man should endeavor to attain something of each. For most, the ideal of bravery, which was the simplest and fairly obvious virtue, was easier to reach; wisdom, most amorphous and complex, was most difficult to acquire. Yet each moral quality constituted a remarkable challenge; each was a goal worthy of accomplishment. Nor were they separate, but rather interdependent. In order to exhibit generosity, for example, bravery and fortitude—conceivably even wisdom—were contributing factors.

The Sioux took scalps, but the practice was outranked as a deed of valor and merit by the *coup*. What the Sioux called a *coup* before the historical period is uncertain. However, both before and after the French came into contact with them, it meant to strike the body of an enemy. The first to deliver the blow was entitled to claim credit for the *coup*. If the feat was accomplished before the enemy was slain, the greater the honor. Every Sioux boy dreamed of counting many *coups*, and thereby acquiring high respect, honors and prestige.

Prior to the arrival of whites on the Great Plains, the Sioux had learned the art of scalping from Indians farther east, who had been taught how to do it by the British during the French and Indian Wars. Scalps, however, were not considered trophies by the Sioux and did not represent battle honors. Normally they were kept only until a scalp dance had been held to celebrate a victory or a successful raid. It was customary for Sioux warriors to give scalps to their womenfolk, who would sew them to small willow hoops which they tied to long poles. After drying them properly in the sun, the women would wave the scalp poles proudly during the scalp dance. Sometimes bits of enemy hairs were saved to fasten onto war shirts or to braid into a person's own locks.

There could have been nothing more colorful and stirring in the early West than the sight of several thousand Sioux in their finest regalia, tanned soft skins painted and decorated, necklaces of bone and shell and elk and grizzly-bear teeth, ornaments of obsidian and quartz, and perhaps turquoise and shells that had passed a thousand or more miles through prehistoric trade channels from the Southwest and the Gulf of Mexico and the Pacific, and garments embroidered with painted quills.*

*Early French traders found abalone and dentalium shells among the Sioux.

The circles of tall skin tepees dotted the grasslands along some
stream, and the columns of smoke from the cooking fires stood up to
the sky by day, and by night the flames burned holes in the darkness,
and the beat of drums and the cries of the dancers rose toward the
stars, shattering the plains silence.

Feathers must be given special mention in such an imaginary scene,
for they not only were used as personal decorations, but were symbolic
of warfare and of religion. Of all primitive Indian artifacts nothing
surpassed in beauty the long war and ceremonial bonnets of the Sioux
of the Great Plains. Invariably they were made of eagle feathers, and
of these the white ones with black tips were the most prized of all,
although some warriors would wear only the feathers of the golden
eagle. Fans made of eagle feathers also were carried in certain dances
and ceremonials. Eagle feathers were attached to buckskin shirts, and
shields were ornamented with them.

On the premise that the Sun Dance involved various forms of
self-torture, it was suppressed by federal statute in 1896. The move
was part of a prolonged attempt by the government to prevent Indians
from practicing their native religion, which was described by hyp-
ocrites in the Indian Bureau—and, of course, by missionary societies
and other church organizations—as barbaric, paganistic, obscene and
animalistic. The Bureau issued a set of regulations called a Code of
Religious Offenses. It was still on the books until 1934, when John
Collier, appointed Commissioner of Indian Affairs by Pres. Franklin
D. Roosevelt, nullified it with a terse order which said: "No interference with Indian religious life or ceremonial expression will hereafter
be tolerated. The cultural liberty of Indians is in all respects to be
considered equal to that of any non-Indian group."

What had the Sun Dance meant for an unknown number of
centuries to the Sioux? Drawing on numerous ethnological sources,
Hassrick answers the question in this way:

> The Sun Dance, by interrelating the various elements of Sioux
> thought, became the epitome of religious expression, culminating
> in supplication by everyone and active sacrifice by the more
> arduous. The quality of the participation exhibited by the Sioux is
> characteristic of their religious fervor—of what some men were
> willing to give of themselves in order to find the true way of life. In
> dancing the Dance in any one of the four forms, the individual
> voluntarily subjected himself to physical suffering for the well-
> being of others. He publicly demonstrated his selflessness by
> submitting to capture, torture, and captivity. Only after enduring
> excruciating suffering could he expect release. In negating the ego,

in denying the drive for self-preservation, the dancer might experience in the fullest sense a resolving of one of the fundamental enigmas of life.

Unlike the Christians who passively revered Christ's example of self-denial through crucifixion and yet profess a comprehension of that denial, the Indian who would purport to understand the implication must himself experience sacrifice physically, mentally, and spiritually. And to be a Sioux, to live life on the best and highest plane, participation in one of the four forms of the Sun Dance was a requisite.

The Sun Dance is still held each year at various Sioux Reservations, and it remains exciting, beautiful and dramatic. For many years self-mortification was omitted from some dances, and suggested rather than practiced in others. In the early 1960s the act of piercing the chest muscles with pegs and breaking loose from thongs attached to the Sun Dance Pole was restored. However, the self-torture features of the present-day ceremony are milder and less bloody than those of past centuries. The Sun Dance was a summer solstice ceremony, and during it considerable sexual license, forbidden at other times, was permitted. Children conceived while it was being held were believed to be especially fortunate, regardless of the legitimacy of their parentage.

In a trading post near Pine Ridge, South Dakota, while chatting casually with several persons about the Sun Dance, the author was given the following prepared statement, which purportedly had been written by a Sioux in the Oglala tribal office:

> The Sun Dance naturally pre-dates Sioux written history, so we do not know when to begin. We do know that it was a form of payment to the Sun God for a prayer that had been answered. The dance was always done in the summer after the hunts had been completed, and the wild berries and fruits dried for the coming winter. The group that was going to do the dance would send a runner from his tribe to the other six tribes of the Sioux Nation, telling of the event, its time and place.
>
> Although the Sun Dance had a strong religious significance these get-togethers often had the air of a fair, with everyone greeting old friends and kinsmen, and the warriors telling of their horse stealing and battles with enemy tribes.
>
> The place where each tribe and each family group of each tribe camped was established by prestige. The full camp when assembled would be in the shape of a curved buffalo horn with the Hunkpapa camping at the head of the horn. After the tribes were in camp, a tall straight tree was chosen by the leader. After a

prayer, it was cut and removed to the dance area. It was not supposed to touch the ground in being moved and decorated before being placed upright in the dance area. The decorations consisted of a toy warrior and a toy buffalo made of skins, a rawhide rope attached to the top of the tree, and a crossarm of limbs and brush. The toy warrior signified the enemies they had fought, the toy buffalo, their dependence on that animal. The rope had a hook on the lower end for hooking onto the flesh of the dancer. The crossarm signified eagles, since the eagles provided them with feathers for decorations.

Each warrior could wear one tipped eagle feather for each coup he had counted against an enemy. Around the tree were placed four colored flags or markers, yellow to the east where the sun rises, red to the south to represent the heat of the noonday sun, black to the west representing the storm clouds that brought rain, and white to the north representing snow.

Before sunrise on the appointed day the dancer or dancers came to the sweat lodge at the east of the dance grounds. The lodge was about four feet high and six feet in diameter, made of sixteen willow limbs placed in the ground and then woven together and covered with a buffalo hide.* A hole was dug in the center of the sweat lodge, and in it were placed heated stones. [Almost always four men participated in this ceremony.] The last man to enter brought a bucket of water and closed the door flap, making it almost airtight. When the water was poured on the hot stones steam resulted, and after a few minutes the purification ceremony was completed.

The dancer lies down, and the medicine man makes an incision in the dancer's chest, and attaches the hook on the leather rope. The dancer arises, backs away from the tree until the rope is taut and dances facing the sun. While dancing he looks at the sun and blows on a turkey wing bone whistle to the beat of the drums. After a few minutes the medicine man who has conducted him to the west, facing east, conducts him to the north facing south, and later to the other points of the compass until he is back facing east. This continues until he is able to tear the hook from his flesh and free himself.

It was a great dishonor not to be able to tear the flesh and be free.

The land of the western Sioux was a magnificent, awe-inspiring, and in many ways an incredibly rich country. It knew extremes of cold and heat, heavy rains and droughts, spectacular storms and destructive winds. Over it ranged game herds comparable in size to any in the

*It was of great importance that sixteen willow limbs be used in making the sweat lodge. See previously where the significance of the number *four* is explained.

primitive world; often its skies were darkened with clouds of wild fowl; there were many fish in its streams; the bounties of its soil were many and diversified.

There were bison moving like great black blankets over the grass combers that beat against the buttes and the valley ridges and the hills and the mountain coasts. There were deer, elk, antelope, bears, cougars, wolves, coyotes, porcupines, foxes, raccoons, squirrels, prairie dogs, skunks, bobcats, badgers, rabbits.

There were for food in the streams, beaver, muskrats, geese, duck, cranes; and there were grouse and prairie chickens, pigeons, whippoor-wills, meadowlarks, magpies, owls, eagles, crows, hawks.

There were wild buffalo berries, cherries, gooseberries, juneberries, strawberries, potatoes, turnips, onions, arrowleaf berries, artichokes, plums, nuts.

If there were shortages and hunger in one place, there was plenty in others. They could move with the game and cache dried foods. The earth was a cold storeroom between December and March, and the springs, summers and autumns were providers of fresh sustenance of innumerable kinds. If the Teton Sioux planted seeds when they were Woodland Indians, they made no effort to farm on the Great Plains. Indeed, it seems that after they had crossed the Missouri River, moving westward, they had forgotten how to grow crops, and lived entirely upon what the gods provided for them.

They moved on to a destiny they believed was theirs, and theirs alone, their economy based on natural forces and products, on battlefield triumphs, on banditry.

> As if to impress upon themselves [writes Hassrick] a constantly positive attitude toward their national fortune, vanity was crystallized in exhibitionism at home and abroad. Risk in battle, to the extreme of overtly courting death, was recognized as among the highest achievements. . . . To exhibitionism was added an aura of violence. Like the Plains country where they lived . . . the Sioux appear to have been a people of severe extremes. To kill an enemy was not enough; often he must be mutilated. To force an enemy tribe into submission was not sufficient; it must be driven from the territory. . . . The Sioux pattern of existence had become so compulsively ingrained in violent self-assertion that there was no turning back. . . . Crescendo followed crescendo in a compounding spiral of action. Yet its climax was never really reached. The collapse of Sioux society came not through an inherent weakness in the system or a failure of the people to meet the demands of

their universe. Rather the course of the denouement struck from beyond anything the Indians could possibly foresee or conceivably control. It came in the form of white conquerors, so unbelievably powerful, so overwhelming in numbers that even the Sioux's most desperate defense was of no avail.

Only one people stood a longer time against American forces, both civilian and military, bent on destroying them—the Apache. When the United States occupied the Southwest by aggression in 1846, the Apache had been fighting the white man for more than two centuries. In 1846, emigrants were crossing the Great Plains, but the greatest migration, as well as the greatest invasion of the Teton Sioux Country, were yet to take place. Strangely, however, the end for both the Apache and the Sioux came at approximately the same time, the sites far apart, in Arizona and Montana.

The identity of the first white man (or men) to meet the Teton Sioux in the northern Great Plains is not, and probably never will be, known. Perhaps the British trader, Henry Kelsey, heard of them, but it seems doubtful that he saw any of them. He was sent in 1690 to induce remote Western tribes to bring their furs to Hudson Bay Company posts. If he met Sioux of the Great Plains, however, it seems doubtful that they were Teton, but rather Assiniboin.

French *voyageurs* pushed far west in Canada, but whether any of them turned southward far enough to reach the Great Plains country of the Teton in the early years of the eighteenth century is not known. That Frenchmen met the Teton in 1742, however, is a historical fact. Louis-Joseph and Francois, sons of the great Canadian trailbreaker and trader, La Vérendrye, in this year, accompanied by only two *voyageurs*, found the Cheyenne, the Teton and the Crow. They crossed the Little Missouri, passed through the Badlands (South Dakota), and forded a stream that would be called Powder River.

On New Year's Day, 1743, the Vérendryes stood on a height in eastern Wyoming, and they saw far to the west a great range of mountains—the Big Horns. They had wanted to go on, believing that from the top of the peaks they would be able to see the Pacific. But Indians (Tetons?) who had joined them somewhere along their trail warned that other white men who had preceded them had been slain.* Louis-Joseph would write that the Indian tale "cooled my ardor considerably for a sea which was already known."

*Undoubtedly a Spanish force coming up from the Southwest.

The brothers Vérendrye turned back, passing through the heart of the Teton Country, crossing the Belle Fourche River, circling the Black Hills and traveling in South Dakota to the Missouri River. In a hillside along the river they buried a metal plate. Inscribed on it besides their own names were the name of the French King and the name of their father, whom they revered, and the date March 30, 1743. In an Indian village near the site they learned to their astonishment that not many days' journey away a Frenchman had been settled for several years, had married a squaw and had a family of half-breeds. Thus it may not be said how long before the time of the Vérendryes *voyageurs* had been living in the Teton Country.*

If the estimates of scientists specializing in demography are accepted as relatively accurate, the early population of the Siouans whose trails were followed in this part totaled more than 58,000 souls.

> Broken down into subdivisions, there were approximately:
> Winnebago (mid-seventeenth century)—4,000
> Hidatsa and Mandan (mid-eighteenth century)—6,100
> Santee tribes (early eighteenth century)—6,500
> Yankton and Yanktonai (mid-nineteenth century)—11,000
> Teton tribes (mid-eighteenth century)—15,000
> Assiniboin (late eighteenth century)—12,000
> Crow (late eighteenth century)—4,000

SOME EXISTING PLACE NAMES

TRIBE	PLACE NAME
Winnebago	Lake and county in Wisconsin. Counties in Illinois and Iowa. Places in Minnesota, Wisconsin, Illinois and Nebraska.
Mandan	City in North Dakota.
Santee	Wahpeton, North Dakota, and Iowa. Sisseton, South Dakota.
Yankton	County and town, South Dakota.
Crow	Absaroka Mountains, Wyoming; Absaroka, North Dakota; Absaroka,

*The plate was buried where Pierre, the capital of South Dakota, would stand, and it was found by some school children in 1913.

	Montana; Crow Creek, Colorado; Crow Creek, Wyoming; Crow River, Minnesota; Crow Agency and Crow Rock, Montana.
Assiniboin	River in Saskatchewan and Manitoba. Assiniboine Peak, British Columbia.
Teton	Brule River, Wisconsin; Brule Lake Station, Ontario; Brule, Nebraska; Brule, Wisconsin; Brule City, South Dakota; Brule Lake, Minnesota; Brule River, Michigan; Oglala, South Dakota; Ogallala, Nebraska; Lakota, Iowa; Lakota, North Dakota.
Dakota Sioux	South Dakota; North Dakota; North Dakota River; South Dakota River; county and town in Nebraska; Sioux Falls, South Dakota; Sioux City, Iowa; Sioux Pass, Montana.

To the Teton Sioux the Black Hills were a "holy land." The region was part of a great reservation assigned for their exclusive occupation under a treaty with the United States. When gold was discovered, the miners and settlers came in hordes, swarming over the Black Hills and the surrounding territory, and the United States conveniently forgot about the terms of the treaty. But the Sioux didn't forget, and their old enemy, the Cheyenne, whom they had once driven out of the country, came to fight beside them against the invaders, and the Black Hills, which are really blue with cloud shadows, were stained with the blood of both red men and white.

Every school boy and girl knows the names of Sitting Bull, and Crazy Horse, and Gall, and Rain-in-the Face and American Horse, but the truth of what they did and why they did it does not always appear in schoolbooks. The heroes of the last wars with the Sioux were not the white pioneers, not the U.S. Cavalry. The heroes were the Teton Sioux, man, woman and child.

Until the last the Sioux fought their white destroyers for their homes and their homelands as they had fought their prehistoric foes, with courage and determination unsurpassed by any people in the history of the world. Their faith in themselves and in their gods was never lost, and although on the battlefield they achieved some notable victories, there were forces they could not fight, that they had no hope of overcoming. For all their bravery, their spirit, their beliefs in themselves, their moral, mental and physical strength, they were helpless in attempting to combat the criminal violations of legal treaties, the wanton disregard of human rights, the breaking of solemn promises, the starvation inflicted upon them by a corrupt political system and a society that, in the way of a faucet, turned standards of decency and justice on and off to serve greed and desire of the moment.

A Selected Bibliography

Alvord, Clarence Walworth, and Lee Bigwood, *The First Explorations of the Trans-Allegheny Regions by the Virginians, 1650–1674*, Cleveland, Ohio, 1912.

Baity, Elizabeth Chesley, *Americans before Columbus*, New York, 1968.

Bancroft, Hubert Howe, *Native Races*, Vols. 1 to 5, San Francisco, 1886–1890.

Benedict, Ruth, *Patterns of Culture*, New York, 1934.

Boas, Franz, *Race, Language and Culture*, New York, 1949.

Brebner, J. B., *Explorers in North America*, London, 1933.

Carley, Kenneth, *The Sioux Uprising of 1862*, Minnesota Historical Society, St. Paul, 1961.

Catlin, George, *Letters and Notes on the Manners and Customs and Conditions of the North American Indian*, New York, 1844.

Chard, C. S., *New World Migration Routes*, College, Alaska, 1958.

Coe, Joffre L., *Cultural Sequence of the Carolina Piedmont in Archaeology*, Chicago, 1952.

Coon, Carlton S., *The Story of Man*, New York, 1962.

Cox, I. J., *The Journeys of La Salle and His Companions*, New York, 1906.

Coxe, Daniel, *A Description of the English Province of Carolina*, Philadelphia, 1750.

De Smet, Pierre Jean (*see* Terrell, *Black Robe*).

De Soto, Hernando (*see* Lewis, T. Hayes).

Dorsey, J. Owen, *Omaha Sociology*, Bureau of American Ethnology, Washington, 1884.

——*Migrations of the Siouan Indians*, American Naturalist, Vol. 20, March, 1886.

——*Osage and Omaha Traditions*, Bureau of American Ethnology, Washington, 1888.

——*Siouan Sociology*, Bureau of American Ethnology, Washington, 1897.

Driver, Harold E., *Indians of North America*, Chicago, 1961.

Ewers, John C., *Indian Life on the Upper Missouri*, Norman, Okla., 1968.

Fletcher, Alice C., and La Flesche, Francis, *The Omaha Tribe*, Bureau of American Ethnology, Washington, 1911.

French, Benjamin Franklin, *Historical Collections of Louisiana*, 7 vols., New York, 1846–1875.

Griffen, James B., *Archaeology of the Eastern United States*, Chicago, 1952.

Hafen, LeRoy R., and Young, Francis Marion, *Fort Laramie and the Pageant of the West, 1834–1890*, Glendale, Calif., 1938.

Haines, Francis, *The Northward Spread of Horses among the Plains Indians*, American Anthropologist, Vol. XL, No. 3, 1938.

Hassrick, Royal B., *The Sioux—Life and Customs of a Warrior Society*, Norman, Okla., 1967.

Hayden, F. V., *Contributions to the Ethnography and Philology of the Indian Tribes of the Missouri Valley*, Philadelphia, 1862.

Hennepin, Louis, *Description of Louisiana*, Minneapolis, Minn., 1938.

Henry, Alexander, and Thompson, David, *New Light on the Early History of the Greater Northwest*, New York, 1897.

Hodge, Frederick W., ed., *Handbook of Indians North of Mexico*, Bureau of American Ethnology, Washington, 1907.

Hopkins, David M., ed., *The Bering Land Bridge*, Stanford, 1967.

Hrdlička, Aleš, *Early Man in America*, Philadelphia, 1937.

Hyde, George E., *A Sioux Chronicle*, Norman, Okla., 1956.

————*Red Cloud's Folk*, Norman, Okla., 1957.

————*Spotted Tail's Folk, A History of the Brulé Sioux*, Norman, Okla., 1961.

————*Indians of the Woodlands*, Norman, Okla., 1962.

————*Indians of the High Plains*, Norman, Okla., 1966.

Irving, Washington, *A Tour of the Prairies*, New York, 1835.

James, Edwin, *Account of an Expedition from Pittsburgh to the Rocky Mountains in 1819 and 1820, Under the Command of Major Stephen H. Long*, Philadelphia, 1823.

Jesuit Relations (*see* Thwaites).

Josephy, Alvin M., Jr., *The Indian Heritage of America*, New York, 1968.

Joutel, Henri (*see* Cox, I. J.).

Kappler, Charles J., *Indian Laws and Treaties*, Washington, 1904.

Kennedy, Michael Stephen (*see* Long, James Larpenteur).

La Flesche, Francis, *The Osage Tribe,* Bureau of American Ethnology, Washington, 1921.

La Potherie, Bacqueville Le Roy de, *Historie de L'Amerique,* Paris, 1722.

Lawson, John, *History of North Carolina,* London, 1714.

Lederer, John, *The Discoveries of John Lederer in Several Marches from Virginia to the West of Carolina,* 1669–1670 (in Alvord, q.v.).

Lewis, Meriwether, and Clark, William, *Journals,* Elliott Coues, ed., New York, 1893.

Lewis, T. Hayes, ed., *The Narrative of the Expedition of Hernando De Soto by the Gentleman of Elvas* (in *Spanish Explorers in the Southern United States*), New York, 1959.

Long, James Larpenteur, *The Assinboines,* Michael Stephen Kennedy, ed., Norman, Okla., 1961.

Long, Stephen H. (*see* James, Edwin).

Lowie, Robert H., *The Crow Indians,* New York, 1935.

——*Indians of the Plains,* New York, 1954.

——*Primitive Society,* New York, 1961.

McGowan, Kenneth, *Early Man in the New World,* New York, 1950.

McGuire, J. D., *Pipes and Smoking Customs of American Aborigines,* Washington, 1897.

Mangelsdorf, P. C., and Reeves, R. G., *The Origin of Indian Corn and Its Relatives,* College Station, Texas, 1939.

——and Smith, C. Earle, Jr., *New Archaeological Evidence on Evolution in Maize,* Cambridge, Mass., 1949.

Mannypenny, George W., *Our Indian Wards,* Cincinnati, Ohio, 1880.

Marriott, Alice, *The First Comers,* New York, 1960.

Martin, Paul S., Quimby, George I., and Collier, Donald, *Indians before Columbus,* Chicago, 1947.

Mathews, John Joseph, *The Osages,* Norman, Okla., 1961.

Matthews, Washington, *Ethnography and Philology of the Hidatsa Indians,* Washington, 1877.

Membré, Zenobius (*see* Cox, I. J.).

Meyer, Roy W., *History of the Santee Sioux,* Lincoln, Nebr., 1967.

Nute, Grace Lee, *Caesars of the Wilderness,* New York, 1943.

Parkman, Francis, *La Salle and the Discovery of the Great West*, Boston, 1879.

Powell, John Wesley, *Indian Linguistic Families North of Mexico*, Bureau of American Ethnology, Washington, 1891.

Radin, Paul, *The Winnebago Tribe*, Bureau of American Ethnology, Washington, 1923.

Radisson, Pierre Esprit, *Voyages*, New York, 1943.

Riggs, Stephen Return, *Dakota Grammar, Texts, and Ethnography*, Bureau of American Ethnology, Washington, 1894.

Rights, Douglas, L., *The American Indian in North Carolina*, Durham, N.C., 1947.

Robinson, Doane, *History of the Dakota or Sioux Indians*, Minneapolis, 1956.

Roe, Frank Gilbert, *The Indian and the Horse*, Norman, Okla., 1955.

Royce, Charles C., *Indian Land Cessions in the United States*, Bureau of American Ethnology, Washington, 1899.

Sandoz, Mari, *Crazy Horse*, Lincoln, Nebr., 1942.

Shea, John Gilmary, *Discovery and Exploration of the Mississippi Valley*, New York, 1853.

———*Early Voyages up and down the Mississippi*, Albany, N.Y., 1861.

Shetrone, H. C., *The Mound Builders*, New York, 1930.

Skinner, Alanson, *Ethnology of the Ioway Indians*, Milwaukee, Wis., 1926.

Smith, John, *The True Travels, Adventurers and Observations of Captaine John Smith*, Richmond, Va., 1819.

Speck, Frank G., *Tutelo Rituals*, Chapel Hill, N.C., 1935.

Swanton, John R., *The Indian Tribes of North America*, Bureau of American Ethnology, Washington, 1952.

Tabeau, Pierre-Antoine, *Narrative of Loisel's Expedition to the Upper Missouri*, Norman, Okla., 1939.

Terrell, John Upton, *Furs by Astor*, New York, 1963.

———*Black Robe*, New York, 1964.

———*Traders of the Western Morning: Aboriginal Commerce in Pre-Columbian America*, Southwest Museum, Los Angeles, 1967.

———*La Salle*, New York, 1968.

———*American Indian Almanac*, New York, 1971.

———*Land Grab*, New York, 1972.

Thomas, Cyrus, *Report of the Mound Exploration*, Bureau of American Ethnology, Washington, 1894.

Thwaites, Reuben Gold, *Jesuit Relations and Allied Documents, 1610–1791*, 73 vols., Cleveland, 1896–1901.

Townsend, Cyrus (*see* Quapaw in Hodge).

Underhill, Ruth M., *Red Man's Religion*, Chicago, 1965.

Webb, Walter Prescott, *The Great Plains*, New York, 1931.

Wedel, Waldo R., *Prehistoric Man on the Great Plains*, Norman, Okla., 1961.

Wormington, H. M., *Ancient Man in North America*, Denver, 1958.

Index